YOUR SOUL MAP

LIBERATION, HUMAN DESIGN, AND THE BIPOC EXPERIENCE

AYCEE BROWN AND
ASHA D RAMAKRISHNA

Copyright © 2023 by Aycee Brown and Asha D Ramakrishna

Your Soul Map
Liberation, Human Design, and the BIPOC Experience

All rights reserved.
No part of this work may be used or reproduced, transmitted, stored, or used in any form or by any means graphic, electronic, or mechanical, including but not limited to photocopying, recording, scanning, digitizing, taping, Web distribution, information networks or information storage and retrieval systems, or in any manner whatsoever without prior written permission from the publisher.

The Quantum Human Design™ language and Human Design charts in this book are copyrighted by Karen Curry Parker and used with permission.

In this world of digital information and rapidly changing technology, some citations do not provide exact page numbers or credit the original source. We regret any errors, which are a result of the ease with which we consume information.

An Imprint for GracePoint Publishing (www.GracePointPublishing.com)

GracePoint Matrix, LLC
624 S. Cascade Ave. Suite 201
Colorado Springs, CO 80903
www.GracePointMatrix.com
Email: Admin@GracePointMatrix.com

SAN # 991-6032

A Library of Congress Control Number has been requested and is pending.

ISBN: (Paperback) 978-1-955272-64-3
eISBN: 978-1-955272-65-0

Books may be purchased for educational, business, or sales promotional use.
For bulk order requests and price schedule contact:
Orders@GracePointPublishing.com

I dedicate this book to all the Black, Brown, girls, and women who want to explore Human Design and felt it might not be for them... It is for you. You belong in this space.

Aycee Brown

This book is in many ways is my way to honor and thank the ancient traditions and their peoples. To the ancestors who have preserved these traditions and to the generations to come that reclaim their rightful place in the teachings preserved by people who have been oppressed. At a personal level I dedicate this to my daughters, Sarada and Dharma, and to their *Papi Glen,* my life partner, and the man who encourages us to be our authentic powerful selves. These three humans have been my real teachers in deeply understanding the archetypes that live within so many aspects of the Human Design system, and of course have informed my path in life and business.

Asha D Ramakrishna

Table of Contents

Foreword v
Introduction vii
Why This Book and Why Now xiii
How to Use This Book xix
Human Design from Our Lens xxi

Part 1: Decolonization and Altered Origins of Human Design

    Human Design from Their Lens 1
    The Mask of Conditioning 9
    The Culture of the Human Design Community 13

Part 2: Origins and Systems of Culture in Human Design

    Honoring the Parts to Make the Parts Whole 21
    How to Trust Human Design in an Unsafe World 57

Part 3: Integration and Equity of Human Design

    Meeting Yourself with a New Lens 65

Part 4: Adaptation and Embodiment in Human Design

    Capitalism and the Promise of a New Economy 105
    Freedom to Manage in Professional Spaces 113

Part 5: The Charts from a BIPOC Perspective

    Understanding Your Chart 119

    Human Design Aura Types Redefined 121

    Profiles and I Ching 145

    The Intersection of the Human Design Chart: Use It for Your Exaltation 153

Bringing It All Together 189

Contributors from Our Interviews 191

About the Authors 197

Foreword

There's a big elephant in the Human Design room that we don't often talk about.

Human Design is a synthesis of Eastern (Vedic) and Western astrology, the Chinese I Ching, the Hindu chakra system, Judaic Kabbalah, and quantum physics. And while the system itself is a synthesis that makes it into a whole new creation, Human Design often ignores its cultural roots, glossing over those components. Maybe that's because Human Design is young—younger than many reading this—and with most everything else in life, it takes time to mature, to grow, and get back to its origin.

We are waking up to the fact that we must deeply honor and respect the culture and practices of people and become cognizant that integrated patterns exist deeply embedded within groups of people that are as true and real and important as the choices they make. We must acknowledge the origins—the roots and foundation—of the synthesized parts of Human Design and the parts of the chart containing elements of spiritual practices or cultural identity. It is important that we acknowledge and respect the origin of each facet and extend our gratitude and honor instead of simply taking and making use of without authority or right.

The beauty of humanity is that we are a giant cosmic puzzle with billions of utterly unique and non-duplicable pieces. We are simultaneously an individual piece of the puzzle and an integral part of the whole. Appreciate the different pieces, explore and learn from them, savor them, but do your best to make sure that they stay protected and in integrity.

Human Design teaches us that we are all different. We all have our own experiences and inner wisdom that we bring to the table. There is no "one way" to share Human Design.

As this powerful system grows in popularity, it is vital we remind ourselves that the purpose of Human Design is to help people remember their own inner authority to find their own way and truth. We must continue to expand, mature, and grow in the ways that we use Human Design as a tool for liberation. We must also remember that even though, at the heart, there are core elements of our human story that inextricably entangle and unify us, we are all unique, vital beings with very different histories and experiences. Human Design reminds us that there are an infinite number of paths and truths to our soul curricula.

Thank you, Asha and Aycee, for bringing this painful and closeted conversation to the forefront and for helping us remember that our true beauty is in our diversity and in the full expression of who we are.

Karen Curry Parker
March 2023

Introduction

When we started out on this journey, we wanted to create a book that showed Human Design from a Black, Indigenous, and People of Color (BIPOC) lens and perspective, and frankly, our disposition was one of disdain and anger. This sacred rage fueled the motivation to birth a book into the world that could make the wrongs right. In the process, we have come to realize that the voices and experiences that we heard through the interviews and through our own synthesis have become a love letter to Human Design and humanity and have also allowed us to see the system with appreciation and understanding of its evolution. We now want to dissect the system from a lens of appreciation and investigation and see how a beautiful system can also have harmful roots, and how we, as stewards of such a system, have a desire and influence to create space through language to heal its roots. It is a living system, and as such, it has room to evolve and adapt to better serve the whole. We recommend you have your Human Design chart at hand to reference as you read this book. You can get your free chart at www.geneticmatrix.com.

Like any other system, there are always two sides to a coin; there are those who want to maintain the system and those who want to evolve it. We can see how purists have a deep respect for the origins of any holistic framework, and how precious the preservation of the origins of Human Design is in maintaining integrity. It is like somebody creating naked goat yoga without giving proper reverence to an entire healing system of yoga and all its limbs; we understand that yoga itself needs to evolve with humanity; can this be done while honoring the roots of such a sacred lineage? We believe that similarly, Human Design can both be honored, revered, critiqued, adjusted, and reborn to meet the needs of an evolving human experience. Anything that has a great foundation must evolve; that is the nature of all things that serve. The era of having BIPOC modify systems that are created by and for non-BIPOC (consciously or not) needs to cease. We are in a time where we can evolve and also prioritize those who have been marginalized by society; now is the time. What is not always understood is that this is not only about doing the right thing, it is also about shifting our attention toward the liberation of those least encouraged to be liberated; that is how we make Human Design better.

One of the most healing interviews we had through this process was with Karen Curry Parker. Karen is one of the OG Teachers of evolving Human Design, especially for Gen X and Millennials. Many of us have learned Human Design through her lens, and it is an important one to understand. Karen has a cultural and spiritual background in Judaism and Kabbalah, which has influenced her work in ways that differentiate her from her original teacher, Ra Uru Hu. Karen knew Ra on a personal level since she worked in his organization and studied with him extensively before his passing. This gives her insight into the original system, the founder, and the need for change. Her voice in the community has been imperative for many of us who needed a woman's perspective, and her compassionate nature (Gate 50) has offered a space of integrative healing and the embodiment of the Human Design system. What we know today is that the way she has been teaching is rooted in the ethos of the Kabbalah (more on this later). Just as Karen repositioned the teachings of Human Design with the Judaic foundation, we also want to introduce the other foundations that make Human Design and open the scope so that it can serve BIPOC.

In Karen's words:

> "One of the core tenets of Judaism is a principle called Tikkun Olam, which means our role in each generation is to move ourselves toward healing the world; it's our obligation. And I think I would like to see everybody look at their Design as a soul curriculum and a path for them to fulfill their obligation, to do their part, and to heal the world." (Karen Curry Parker, personal communication)

The truth is that all of us are in constant negotiation with the world and its demands and aligning to our soul curriculum requires effort. In many ways, this alignment is an individual journey, and you first must be present to your Human Design chart. Explore it, decondition the parts that have seeped in to mold us according to the expectations of the world, and arrive at an understanding that allows us to embody the pieces that belong to us. Living out our individual soul curriculum and helping each other do the same seems to be much of what we all hear Karen expressing in everything she does and teaches.

In public discourse, the integrity and character of Ra, the founder of Human Design, is very much in question. Many of us wrestle with perpetuating a system that was created by a white man that seemed to have had controversial ethics. Many modern-day spiritual leaders who carry transformational wisdom have displayed moral dissonance, making many of us question the validity of the teachings they hold. Yet, we see how the teachings help us, so we struggle to make sense of endorsing their channeled wisdom. We do believe that it is time to hold leaders to greater standards of behavior, and part of the reason for investing our time and energy here is to rectify what we can control in Human Design: our own sovereignty within the system.

In comparing Osho[1] to Ra, Karen says:

> "If you can take Osho out of the inspirational quotes, what Osho says is truth with a capital T. How Osho showed up, maybe not so much. I think this has always been my intention with Human Design, to leave the ickiness behind. There's truth in Human Design, but the people part is kind of messy.
>
> "To a certain degree, I think it's okay that the people part is messy, as long as we can see it and we don't defend it. I think that in the beginning especially when you go back and you read, say *The Book of Lines* or *The Book of Changes*, or *The Black Book*

---

[1] https://en.wikipedia.org/wiki/Rajneesh

when Ra originally downloaded his initial experience with The Voice, his love for humanity was palpable. Like I literally can't read sections of it without crying because I'm so moved by how beautiful the story of humanity is when Ra started transmitting this system; he had seven years of a transit that brought him Sacral definition.

"And then the Gate 5 moved out and his Sacral got open. All of a sudden, all that energy just went away. He no longer had Sacral definition. That's all his energy to the Throat. He had children, he had some unprocessed trauma. I look at him with, Kavod[2]. A Jewish principle of compassion.

"When I look at him with compassion, I'd say he was a vessel for a brilliant system. He was a beautifully flawed human being and everything that he shared was processed through his filter. You have to disengage from his filter and make it your own. We try to look at it with compassion. That's all I can say because otherwise, I get mad. I am not mad at Ra. That's the thing, I'm not mad at Ra. I think Ra was flawed, profoundly flawed. I'm mad at people who perpetuate the mythology of Ra, especially those people who know better." (Karen Curry Parker, pers. comm.)

Similar to how much the spiritual communities have taken the truth in teachings and set aside the humans who steward the teachings, we want to create a space where Human Design gets to flourish outside of one human. Then

---

[2] Kavod: compassion. https://jewishjournal.com/culture/176189/

it can be handed to those who want to heal the fractured pieces, re-indigenize the parts, and allow the system to evolve and mutate in service to humanity. Especially communities that need it most.

Why This Book and Why Now

You are here to be the highest form of who you are and nothing else. Love that. [3]

—Asha Ramakrishna

With all the information about Human Design on the internet and in books, and all the mythologies about the system, there is still a lack of BIPOC representation and communion. What we have come to realize is that Human Design is a beautiful system that can provide personal autonomy and freedom to oneself while on your soul's journey. The teachings of the system, however, are limited by the identity and experience of the leading Human Design teachers. This is at no fault to them, but the current educational Human Design models lack the depth and richness of Black, Indigenous, and People of Color. We believe that when we liberate those that are oppressed the most in our world, we liberate all.

---

[3] *The Priestess Code: Awakening the Modern Woman* by Asha D Ramakrishna.

One example to help us see how this path to liberation can work is tuning in to the notion that:

> "Until Black Women Are Free, None of Us Will Be Free."[4]
>
> —Barbara Smith

In the spiritual community, there is an undertone of assimilation that doesn't allow BIPOC to feel safe enough to bring the entirety of our experiences and lineage to these systems. As BIPOC, we often feel as though we have to take what is and be okay with it and modify these systems to fit us without the support of non-BIPOC leaders. That brings an us-versus-them mentality and isolates our existence. This highlights the necessity to deepen a body of work to meet us in our current reality and allow us to fulfill our truest potential. Human Design is a soul map that allows us to stay in alignment with who we truly are. For BIPOC, experiencing our truth has been stripped away over time, and systems like this can help us come back to our souls in the truest form.

The era of code-switching[5] our soul's journey and ancestral experience is over. We no longer want to deny our rightful place and power in the world. Many of us have been told that we aren't worthy; worthy of love, worthy of wealth, worthy of freedom, or anything that's good in the world. Yet we persevere and continue to fight for a fraction of what is available to us. This is no longer our desired reality and

---

[4] https://www.newyorker.com/news/our-columnists/until-black-women-are-free-none-of-us-will-be-free
[5] Code-Switch is altering our language and culture depending on environments https://en.wikipedia.org/wiki/Code-switching

many of us aren't going to lay down and just take what has been given to us. We want more, we demand more, and we are creating sacred spaces so that those who look like us can thrive as much as anyone else.

The highest expression of a human being is visible through the Human Design map. We are able to see the unique expression of our soul and life curriculum, and we are able to ground in the areas of our gifts and our challenges. When we divorce ourselves from the expectations of society, our DNA, capitalism, our families, religions, and everyday life, we are able to drop into having a life partnership with our incarnate soul, the unique expression of who we are. This divorce or deconditioning as we call it in the Human Design community takes work and time. Ideally, it is held in a sacred space. The inherent limitless model in Human Design allows for an organic liberation of the individual. The reason we want to bring this system to so many people is that it has given us the freedom to exist in this crazy world. When we allow the mystery of the chart to commune with us, we are grounded in our own sense of self without boundaries and with a sense of all doors opening for us because we are who we are and nothing else.

The system is good and benefits us all, yet there is a lack of acknowledgment for its parts and the unethical makings of the system. Human Design comprises Western and Vedic astrology, the Hindu chakra system, the Jewish Kabbalah, the Chinese I Ching, and metaphysics. Some current-day Human Design teachers and enthusiasts do not acknowledge these parts and overlook the history of these systems that make Human Design rich with the support of these worldwide spiritual traditions. We cannot forget that for thousands of years, priests, priestesses, medicine people, householders, and everyday people dedicate themselves to preserving wisdom through rituals, ceremonies, research, apprenticeship, teaching, learning, translating, and embodiment of esoteric teachings in everyday life. These traditions are alive because civilizations have dedicated themselves to preserving them and passing them from generation to generation and this devotion merits great reverence and respect.

It is true that we do not need to have a depth of knowledge in the parts (the traditions) to be able to practice our Strategy. The greatest gift in decision-making—laid out for us in the chart but ignoring all these time-tested ancient wisdoms—miss the mark on the depth and breadth that each millennial teaching can offer to the self-realization process. We invite all to step into cultural humility and trust that by doing so, we benefit at an individual level while creating space for a true honoring of the traditions that existed before Human Design. In many ways, these ancient teachings make it possible for Human Design *to* exist. Human Design sits on the shoulders of time-practiced and honored teachings.

We can't love a system and ignore or whitewash the things that don't sit well with us as BIPOC individuals. We cannot afford that ignorance. We must address and correct the parts that make up Human Design (Western and Vedic astrology, the Hindu chakra system, etc.) and honor them for the true magic they hold while embracing how they complete this system. We want to bring forth the truths and amend the practices within these parts before we can truly embrace Human Design as a whole.

A component that has come to light in our world and is slowly seeping into spiritual communities, goes beyond cultural appropriation and into the re-education and re-indigenization of each of us, especially BIPOC. We have ancestry that not only has gone through trauma but also has experienced abundance, community support, joy, and a deep connection to the unseen realms; it's time we create space for the reclamation of our wise lineages.

This book is part love letter and part reframe to a system that has given us so much yet has also asked us to continue to oppress and perpetuate the construct of whiteness and privilege. In many ways, the Human Design community and its leaders have historically disregarded systemic trauma and the BIPOC experience. We aim to shift the lens of this beautiful system and reframe how we use it. We ask that you read this with an open heart and an open mind knowing that yes, there are some questionable actions from Human Design's origins; however, what this system can offer us is beyond one person or group within the community. Look at this as an opening to a new way of experiencing the world, where we are truly free.

How to Use This Book

This book has five parts, and each part goes over specific information that will take you on a journey to understanding Human Design and its origins as well as different perspectives from industry peers and skeptics.

In part one, we discuss the current state of the Human Design community, where it started and how the system was taught, and where it's going with the new infusion of more diverse people being exposed to the system.

In part two, we break down the origins of the parts of Human Design that make the system whole and normally get overlooked by a modern lens that doesn't have full reverence for Indigenous wisdom. We also express our views in how to evolve what an actual safe space means in this spiritual modality.

In part three, we give our perspective of how we see each Human Design Aura Type and why it looks different for BIPOC. You will see that we give space to the BIPOC experience and why Human Design from our lens needs more nuance because of our lived experiences and of our ancestors as people in this world.

In part four, we discuss how to thrive in this economy and in work environments and how we will uniquely evolve as the world and humanity evolves.

In part five, we give you the tools to use Human Design as a practical solution to the realities we face as BIPOC. This section serves as an easy-to-search reference guide that you can use to answer general questions about yourself and support other people in your life.

We also infuse interviews throughout the book that support and give diverse perspectives from leaders in the industry.

Human Design from Our Lens

Asha's Human Design Story

Short of taking my daughter to a Mayan *curandera* (shaman) in Guatemala, I would have done anything to bring more peace and harmony to our home. In many ways, life was more than I could handle for many years. We would go through a cycle of peace at home and then, without warning, my daughter would have an explosive outburst, causing us all to spin into survival mode. Her sensitivity to the tension in our marriage, the mixing of energies from living in the city, and her own undiagnosed anxiety, caused us to get real and pause to be present to what she was signaling to us.

I thought I was a hippie mama (feeding her organic foods before that was a mainstream thing, using essential oils and giving massages before it was common practice), but this child's nervous system was *not* regulated, and we were walking on eggshells trying to keep her happy. I eventually put down my dreams of having a career when I realized she was a full-time job.

I confessed my agony to a friend who responded, "have you tried Human Design?" This was in 2005 and Human Design was almost unknown. Given my desperation, I signed up for a family session. Originally it was to understand my oldest daughter and to help me cope with having a second newborn daughter, yet slowly it unfolded into a way of helping my struggling marriage, myself, and the way I did business, eventually becoming a pivotal tool in my business consulting work.

When I found out my oldest daughter, Dharma, was a Reflector, the correct perspective fell into place; this was not about her, it was about us healing the dynamic so that she could reflect back a healthy family community. The family session led to a three-month Parenting Coaching class with my now-friend Karen Curry Parker and to the beginning of a life with the lens of this system. This has allowed me to raise two very different spirited daughters, thrive and grow with my partner of twenty plus years, and live an abundant life.

Human Design was not the answer for the big healing job at hand, but it was the context by which we approached our understanding of what had been buried (or at least hidden) from the surface of the day-to-day. Understanding the role of my Reflector daughter helped me to focus on creating a community (family) that was healthy. My priority became healing my angry inner-child and the resentment I projected onto my partner. I vowed to not hide from the inner work and this dedication allowed me to eventually heal my mother and father wounds.

Dharma (at nineteen) writes:

> "Having a constant flow of foreign energy was not only exhausting but also alienating. Not understanding why I was feeling any which way drove me to question myself and since I was too young to articulate these complex emotions, I expressed myself as any child does: with unrelenting rage. I was so confused and hurt inside due to emotions that weren't even my own most of the time. Having this knowledge ten, fifteen years later, I have finally found an explanation and can manage my feelings and life more effectively." (Dharma Cooper, pers. comm.)

As a 4/1 Manifesting Generator, going deep with Human Design came easy once I embodied my Strategy. I know many people jump in and learn everything, but I was a bit slower into the system; I embodied first, then learned. For nearly seven years I focused on my Strategy, not because it was a methodical process but because astrology and the system overwhelmed me. Then slowly I started diving into the mechanics of how we affect each other's auras and understanding my relationship with my partner. Being married to a 3/5 Generator has its challenges and Human Design helped me to accept and surrender to our dynamic without resisting the natural flow.

I remembered the moment that solidified my embodiment. I had been asked to be a part of a million-dollar coaching platform to be the in-house Human Design teacher. My strategic brain was fully aligned, but my Sacral was giving me a big no. I was so disappointed, but I made a choice "If I'm going to be teaching this system, I have to fully follow it and live it." I listened to my Sacral while my mind kicked and screamed. I'm not sure what happened, but a couple of weeks later, the rest of me settled and I was glad I had said no. Ever since that moment, I may debate my Sacral, but I do what she says. I've come to learn that my Sacral represents more than just a Strategy, and is a way into pleasure, rewilding, and my power. That moment made me the teacher I am today.

Why this book and why now? Post-2020 we all became aware of the changes we needed to make as a collective: heal systemic racism and give people the tools to heal and thrive in life and business. However, I was fortunate to have had a jump-start on my inner decolonizing work when I met Trudi Lebrón at a conference in Portland, Oregon in 2017. We talked about the inequalities in schools and in business. Fast forward to 2018 when I enrolled in her program along with her co-facilitator Weeze Doran to understand the sociological impact of colonization in modern life. This work began to rattle my approach to living and to business. I began questioning everything I had subscribed to and finally validated the discrimination I felt as an immigrant from Venezuela but had shoved under the rug in order to move forward in life. I enrolled in another decolonizing container with Weeze and the lens of life has not been the same since. As you can imagine, once the blinders were off, the sight got wider and being someone who is never shy to express what I witness (Channel 33-13 here!) I got in trouble in all spiritual spaces.

I began questioning the status quo and the minimizing of the system of oppression in Human Design communities, and perhaps the timing was wrong, but my insight and invitation were not well received. I retreated from most spiritual communities, especially the ones led by non-BIPOC, and began coming back to my own roots. My focus became a daily ceremony to the land I live in (occupied Nipmuc territory in Massachusetts) and a re-indigenizing of my Hindu lineage. In light of the events of Black Lives Matter, my Human Design community started to understand why I had been pushing for equity and for conversations that did not minimize the pain and the joy of Black or Indigenous People with Melanin (of Color).

I understand that many of us have epigenetic inheritance (environmentally induced changes to our DNA); basically, we have inherited the lived experience of our ancestors, whether we are aware of it or not, and for most of us, we play those roles of domination or submission without even realizing. The spiritual bypass and micro-aggressions pervading spiritual communities need a serious revamp. Many of us BIPOC have to filter harmful unconscious practices in personal growth and spirituality and make our own assessments of how we integrate these practices. The work environment is another place where we have to armor up to be present, and we are expected to fall in line with extractive corporate and business models and practices just to survive. I stand for the liberation of every human being in every aspect of their lives, and liberation is both an inside job as well as the job of the community at large. This book is a love letter to those of us who want to be validated in our experiences in the world but who also know that tools such as Human Design offer a pathway to our unique, purpose-driven expression.

If I am honest, I am a work in progress. I am not liberated in all ways, but I am walking my talk of practicing the embodiment of my own Design, connecting to the truth that I am the whole chart, and accessing the richness that is available to me as an incarnate being. Human Design to me is practical and can be implemented in business as a model of allowing the individual the unique anointing they receive at the time of birth to fulfill their highest destiny; it is my vision that when we each do this, the whole becomes alive, and the well-being of all sentient beings becomes a reality.

I wanted to partner with Aycee Brown because it is vital that the beautiful voice of Black women be exalted. One of the fun facts is that both Aycee and I devote ourselves to our spiritual growth and our focus is enveloped in our astrological North Node (more on this later). She is a North Node in Leo (the Queen) and I am a North Node in Aquarius (the Priestess). I am here in service to this evolution and revolution and to provide the tools I have researched (unconscious Line 1) and implemented for myself, my family, and my clients (conscious Line 4), for the good of all.

May this work re-indigenize the ancient systems that create the backbone of the Human Design system and may all BIPOC feel more at ease in accessing this potent tool that changed me, my family, and my work.

Aycee's Human Design Story

I must admit when I discovered Human Design, I thought I was in a great place in my life. I'd just moved to a new city with my new boyfriend, and I embarked on a new side hustle in commercial and portrait photography. Prior to moving to the District of Columbia, I'd finished my MBA in marketing and became certified as a life coach. I felt like I had a fresh start and a new lease on life. I was experiencing new love, new creative energy, and new possibilities, but something still didn't feel right. My relationship wasn't quite as fulfilling, and a few things started to surface that I initially ignored. I started feeling alone, again. Growing up in a large family and being the only child was isolating at times. Thanks to my grandmother, I learned to love "being with myself" as she called it. Because of the isolation, even though things moved pretty fast upon my arrival in Maryland, after eight months I found myself laid off and on unemployment. I was devastated. However, this wasn't new to me (having a job and then getting burned out or laid off). Luckily, I always had a side hustle while working in corporate America, and since I was building my photography business it seemed only fitting that I would go and find one of the most popular commercial photographers in the area to see if they had an opening for an internship, and they did. At first it was an amazing experience; unfortunately, the owner had an ego out of this world and treated us like shit. But leave it to the Universe to make my last few weeks on the job life changing.

The resident studio makeup artist and I talked regularly either before shoots or after. She was a huge yogi and into all things spiritual, and it must have been destiny when she excitedly started telling me all about this thing called Human Design. I remember it like it was yesterday. She was packing up her kit and I was cleaning the changing room. I can't remember exactly what we were talking about, but mid-conversation she blurted out "…and I'm a Manifesting Generator." My ears perked up at the word *manifesting* and

I came out of the dressing room. "I'm a Manifestor as well" thinking she was referring to the law of attraction. She said "No, I'm talking about Human Design." At first, I was pissed that I didn't know about it since I was a student of any and all metaphysical tools. She then went on to explain what Human Design was and how she operated in the world. I was intrigued and curious to find out what Type I was. She ran off the list and I just knew I was either a Manifestor or a Manifesting Generator. She told me she would email me the link to get a reading done and I couldn't wait to sign up. I had my call with a lovely woman, and she revealed I was a Projector. I was devastated and I think I almost started crying. She started talking about waiting for the invitation and waiting to be seen and I was pissed off once again. I never waited for anything. I went out and made things happen. That's all I knew.

I come from a family of go-getters, doers, and multi-passionate creatives. We make things happen in my family. After our call, I sat with myself and thought, *Wait… maybe she's right*. Everything that moved forward in my life first came in the form of an invitation. From careers to relationships, to business ventures, they were all invitations. So as always, I went into research mode and went down the Human Design rabbit hole. I would look at websites and videos and practitioners, but I became really confused because no one looked like me. I literally didn't see any Black or Brown people in the system. I was disappointed. I thought, *Here's another system or spiritual tool where everyone in the community doesn't look like me at all*. I was very frustrated, and I made it my mission to learn more about this system. I told a friend about it, and we were going to learn and start teaching Human Design to others.

And so, we began our quest. It soon became clear she wasn't as passionate about it as I was and didn't want to continue. She's a Manifesting Generator and was on to something different. But I wasn't done. I needed to go deeper with it, and I did. I started reading charts for friends, family, coworkers, and my managers, and I was fascinated by the chart and how accurate it was. As a psychic, I was already picking up the information that was in the chart, however, the chart was confirmation.

What I know for sure is that Human Design is Truth. However, the origins are flawed. And it makes it challenging for BIPOC to embrace a system that has flawed origins. My goal in amplifying Human Design is to create a safe space for BIPOC to embrace the system and use this system to advance us as a whole.

As years went by and I continued to embody my Design, I was upset that the system and its community were still very whitewashed. I would watch YouTube videos of people that once again didn't look like me and I couldn't relate. I remember one white man saying that when he is let go from a job, he doesn't look for work. He's a Projector so he just lets the Universe send him a new position. I thought to myself *That's crazy, I could never do that,* and I was right. As a Black woman in America, I couldn't just sit and wait. I couldn't just sit at home and wait for an opportunity to arrive. I had to go out and look for work or create opportunities in spaces that normally I wouldn't see myself in. Then I began to get angry and thought, if this system is so great, which it was, why don't more people who look like me know about it. So, I set out on a mission to make Human Design look like me and flavor it with my experiences and with my life. The more I talk about the system, the more people I help. The more people I help align with a path to help them move toward their truth and destiny, the more I help them become free.

In writing this book we wanted to hear from other BIPOC Human Design practitioners, so we have interviewed Fiona Wong, Jasmine Nnenna, and Clarinda Mann. We also wanted to get perspectives from a Black neurodivergent astrologer, Elmina Bell, who has issues with the Human Design system. In addition, we included Karen Curry Parker because we have learned from her, and she is able to speak to the Kabbalah.

Part 1: Decolonization and Altered Origins of Human Design

Human Design from Their Lens

The Creation of Human Design and Ra's Perspective

According to the foreword in his book *The Human Design System*[6], the founder of Human Design, Robert Alan Krakower, also known as Ra Uru Hu, was penetrated by a "Voice" on January 3, 1987, in Ibiza, Spain. Following that event, he shared "for eight days and nights, I worked, transcribing in detail the Human Design system"[7]. In the first iteration of Human Design, he explains his interpretation of quantum mechanics, the centers, and I Ching hexagrams (as seen in the gates and channels). In 1995 the book *The*

---

[6] The first book written about Human Design.
[7] Quote from *The Human Design System*.

Book of Letters continues with a detailed explanation of definition and circuitry (rave channels), and then later the Types[8], Strategy[9], and Authority[10] were detailed in the book *Human Design: The Definitive Book of Human Design, The Science of Differentiation* by Lynda Bunnell. The years in between, Ra's teachings were primarily through oral tradition.

We admit that we do not have first-hand experience of Ra Uru Hu; all we have are anecdotal stories and perceptions of his language through the books and the videos available. What we do know is that his lens was one of a white Western man who left his family to pursue his spiritual calling and received the downloads in 1987, falling in the Greed Era[11] of the 1980s (1980-1989). We can infer from this that his choices came from great privilege.

When we read Ra's first book, *The Human Design System*, we see that he has condensed and synthesized a translation of the I Ching hexagrams into the gates, yet the process begs the question: What is lost from the original texts? Something that we must all begin to practice as we move into an era of appreciating different cultural teachings, is to seek the foundations of the teachings. What we have seen in spiritual practices such as yoga, is that the teaching of the physical practice, *asana*, traveled to the west in many ways

---

[8] Types: Manifestor, Manifesting Generator, Generator, Projector, Reflector.
[9] Strategy: Initiate, Respond, Invitation, Lunar Cycle.
[10] Authority: Sacral, Emotional, Splenic, Ego/Heart, Self/Identity/G, Mental/Environmental, Lunar.
[11] Greed Era: https://www.latimes.com/archives/la-xpm-1994-11-13-tm-62250-story.html; https://hbr.org/1992/01/crime-greed-big-ideas-what-were-the-80s-about

without the foundation of Hindu philosophy. This has resulted in a practice void of its roots, and much is lost in translation.

Therefore, our critical lens urges us to now have a deeper understanding of the roots in the Human Design system so we can really embody and help others with the depth of the transmission that lies in the stories of the I Ching for example, without trivializing or whitewashing their meaning. Their meaning can be summarized in a word but simplifying it in this way can lose the relationship we have to each hexagram. To embody a hexagram, or a gate in Human Design, is to know its story, to sit with the story, and to practice the story so it becomes our own.

Given his privileged and limited cultural perspective of the parts of the system (I Ching, Hindu chakra system, Kabbalah, and even tropical and Vedic astrology), we aim to re-root and re-acclimate the parts to liberate and make Human Design accessible to those with less privilege.

The Audacity of Being Ra

Fiona Wong is a 3/5 Projector, writer, and Human Design practitioner of Chinese descent commenting on the stories that surround Human Design and the way that representation can matter when there's a question of appropriation.

> "I get exhausted with the phrase 'that's what Ra said,' or 'Ra was designed to shock.' I actually took one of their classes—the Human Design School's classes—and recall there was something in one of the textbooks that says the liver does not

regenerate, which is why it's important to take care of your G Center.

"And that's just not true, the liver does regenerate itself. So I asked the instructor, why does it say that in a textbook? Why do you continuously teach something even though scientifically and biologically, it is not true? And she said to me, 'you have to remember that Ra was designed to shock. So, he said that to shock people into not drinking a whole lot and destroying their liver.'

"And I said, 'But isn't Ra—his reputation—wasn't he a big drinker? He talks about tripping on LSD in some of his texts.' So that's why I feel like we can't just depend on the word of this one person. I love Karen Curry Parker. I feel like she gets a lot of backlash because she does rename some stuff and she has her own interpretation of the system.

"And for me, it's like, Thank you. Thank you for giving us a different perspective. I love reading a lot of independent bloggers like people on Instagram because they're sharing glimpses of their life. I don't feel like Human Design can be learned from a textbook. When I teach Human Design to other people, I call it field training. We're going to dive into it. Let's get your family member, let's read their chart. It's not just about deciphering it. Now that I've told you some of the pieces of your chart, I want to hear your story. I want you to flavor the rest of the chart. And that's why I feel like we can't just say Ra said this or Ra said that.

"Cool. But what about the person we're reading for? What are they saying? What stories are they bringing to the table and how do they identify? And we can learn so much from that. There's limitless knowledge and understanding and wisdom there.

"I think the big part was also—I have bipolar disorder and I've been institutionalized. If I said the things that Ra said, or if I openly admitted to that much psychedelic use or talked about 'downloading' something in Ibiza—if I did this, if any of us did, we would be in a mental institution; people would laugh at us. People would call us frauds and we would dishonor our families if we dared do something like that.

"I wrote this blog post asking the question: Is Human Design cultural appropriation? And for me, I feel like I can't necessarily answer that question, but whether or not it is appropriation, if I come forward with my voice in Human Design—if we come forward with our voices and we are supporting our communities and reaching out to groups who normally don't have access to this, and we are creating that space for ourselves, whether or not it is appropriation, we are able to take it back, and we are also able to re-flavor it with people that look like us.

"I used to get a little shaken up when I would get emails from people that would say 'I've never seen someone who's Chinese do Human Design.' And when I first got those emails, I felt this was a problem. That's not okay because there are just some things that are in a cultural context, gender identity, or another context that not every Human Design reader can just go ahead and work with. And I feel like there are also not a lot of people who are trauma-informed or who have done trauma training working in Human Design.

"You can't just tell someone to upheave everything they've learned in their life, all their ancestral traditions, everything they learned in their household, and just be like, well, you're a Projector, or you're a Manifestor—do whatever (the Strategy for each Type). There's a lot of context missing and because people like us are not as vocal or we're not as heard in these systems, our contexts are not necessarily brought to the table.

"I think that's why we have to show up. And that's why even when people talk shit to women or join Facebook groups and just trash Human Design readings—we gotta be resilient. It sucks.

"Someone wrote a book, it was a white man, that said 'you're being conditioned when you're around people, but you're being influenced when you're not in their presence.' I feel like it's gotta be more than that. What if we're talking to someone on the internet? What if we're reliving a memory and they're not physically with us anymore? We don't have words for these things from the official school. So I feel like expanding our vocabulary and expanding the experiences we are listening to makes a big difference." (Fiona Wong, pers. comm.)

We asked Fiona to address the hierarchy of Authority,[12] spoken about from the Traditional Human Design perspective, such as Manifestors having the most power in the world, etc.

> "I don't use the hierarchy of Authority at all, because I don't think it's helpful. I understand, we're going to use the excuse that Manifestors come from a place where hierarchy is a thing, and that's how he (Ra) sees the world. As a Projector presenting the system that does not benefit me, and I don't think it benefits my clients at all.
>
> "I do really enjoy the explanation of auras [Types] because I think it ties everything together. With a Projector for example, who needs to wait for an invitation as part of their Strategy, I use the words piercing and penetrating because that comes with the word consent and it helps a lot of my clients understand: 'your aura is so direct and piercing, that the other person needs to consent, and that is your invitation.'
>
> "I like using auras to tie it all together, but not anything that's hierarchical. I don't even like to tell someone like, 'you have a rare Type' or 'you have some sort of rarity' because rarity doesn't really mean anything. What's your story? How do you flavor this rarity? How do you flavor this Authority? So that's how I feel about it.

---

[12] *The Definitive Book of Human Design*, Lynda Bunnell and Ra Uru Hu, page 106.

"I think the only really big thing is that we're all just continuations of what came before us, and that includes our place in Human Design. We're a continuation of whatever the system began as. We're furthering it. Don't go backward." (Fiona Wong, pers. comm.)

The Mask of Conditioning

Conditioning is a term that is used in Human Design to explain how most of us have been trained to follow a program given to us by parents and culture.

There is an oversimplification of the concept of conditioning in the Human Design community. This means that there is a belief that we are all affected equally by family, society, and epigenetic changes without accounting for the fact that the history of each person is more than just the individual, it is also based on and affected by previous generations, systematic oppression, racism, trauma, and past lives. The current system favors cis white men at the top of the food chain. It is common for Human Design to look at conditioning as one-dimensional and not account for the fact that each of us, especially BIPOC, has a history of colonization that makes our experience vastly different from everyone else's. So to label our pain and trauma as *conditioning* is wrong because it is so much more than that.

We have seen this oversimplification to be harmful to BIPOC individuals when practitioners do not have the skill set, background, or ethics to understand the lived experience of BIPOC. This is how the tools that can help us become gatekeeping practices. In the spirituality community, including Human Design, when someone is not affected by something there is an ignorance of why it matters. Overriding the importance of the BIPOC experience creates harm when there is a lack of consideration for the individual perspective. This then becomes exploitation and creates a sense of hierarchy in spiritual communities.

There are many examples of how spiritual leaders abuse their power, knowingly or unknowingly. In many instances, it is due to the lack of education around power dynamics in our world, and the hidden trauma BIPOC face. It is also important to highlight that as BIPOC, we heal differently.

At the expense of creating a monolith of all BIPOC, many of us have an inner drive to heal so that we can feel safe in the world. This is a different hurdle than someone who is not discriminated against for their skin color. The challenges are *not* the same, therefore it is hard for someone who has not experienced consistent obstacles due to the way they look to understand; a cis white man or woman cannot understand the challenges of a Black trans person. Many in our spiritual circles may have had challenges but the challenges are not the same. This is not about creating hierarchy in pain, but more to highlight blind spots pervading our communities. Utilizing a blanket statement of conditioning can be harmful, and we each deserve to be in spaces that understand the nuances of race and cultural identity.

The Culture of the Human Design Community

Ra was a white man who received the Human Design download; we acknowledge him for being the conduit. Now, let's take a closer look at this scenario. Ra was a man who left his family behind. In general, as BIPOC, we have challenges with that because we are taught to be community and family centric. So, this initiates a moment of pause for many of us. Ra did a beautiful job explaining the I Ching in his first book; however, as oral traditions would tell us, the story of each of the hexagrams is pivotal to embodying their energy and message. Unfortunately, people that are non-descendants of these philosophies fail to realize that the origins and old ways of teaching such tools are important to their essence. There's an underlying tone that this system was created out of thin air, and ownership is in question. Typically, when ownership is nebulous, the one with the most power claims it. This evokes questions around ethics, cultural humility, and a critical lens for examining what most cis white Western men and women do in this scenario. Did he seek teachers and elders from the cultures represented in Human Design?

The culture in the Human Design community is to either worship all of his teachings as Truth or revere the teachings of others who are interested in evolving the work. The nuance of who gets to be a teacher and who does not is an important conversation. Is proximity to Ra the marker? Or is embodiment of the whole chart after working with it for over fifteen years more valid? We each get to decide.

Certifications, Training, and Ethics

Certifications and training are valuable models of education; however, we need to understand that there are socioeconomic barriers that most non-BIPOC have historically not considered when pricing or structuring their programs. Many non-BIPOC feel like they don't have to, but a lot of their practices and principles, specifically in spiritual spaces including Human Design, do not originate from their own cultures. For instance, yoga has become a practice catered and financially positioned for those with disposable income and those from South Asian countries have limited access to these trainings and practices. Most yoga teacher trainings in the US are led by white teachers and yoga schools and have a population of mostly white students. In addition to this intrinsic exclusive practice, the original culture rarely benefits financially from these ventures; few yoga teacher trainings offer reparation or equity seats, nor do they send money to temples in India.

According to Trudi Lebrón in her book *The Antiracist Business Book* on the scale of average wealth using households with the largest wealth, white households have 6.9 times higher wealth at $983,400 while Black households have $142,500. She also states that in a 2020 second-quarter overview by the Federal Reserve, white households comprise 60 percent of the US population, but have 84 percent of total household wealth, while Black households account for 13.4 percent and only have 4 percent of total household wealth.

There is an ethical obligation for those who hold the most power in any space (no matter their identity) to both honor the cultures that give them the teachings and to also come up with business models that create a spirit of reparations for those who are marginalized. Ethics also plays a role in business practices; many of us have experienced people repurposing our content or teachings without asking for explicit permission. Many of us in spiritual spaces want to share the knowledge and want to also be respected and credited and this does not always happen. As a society, we are hyper-focused on the success of the individual, which is beautiful, but ethical issues arise when we don't credit BIPOC for their original stories and their intellectual property. The experience of BIPOC is nuanced, layered with ancestral origin, and brings so much richness to spiritual practices; when people take them and decide to own them, it robs us of our identity.

Mental Health

The idolization of Human Design as a fix-all can be harmful when we ignore mental health and assume all challenges can be addressed by superimposing the Human Design speak.

For instance, *open centers* are areas in our chart where we pick up energy from our environment and others around us, and we amplify such energy, but we cannot ignore biochemical factors. This can be another way of bypassing the individual's life experiences. Part of why so many of us love Human Design is that it speaks to potential, and we want to amplify that, but we must also be aware that each one of us has situations and circumstances that affect our biochemical makeup and sometimes spiritual practices are not all-encompassing answers.

Even though Human Design's overall message and usefulness are aligned and correct, we still have to acknowledge its inception and the community that has perpetuated the current culture.

Juliet Diaz writes in her book *The Altar Within* about positivity culture in spirituality, the lack of compassion for the experience of those who are struggling, and how harmful this is to BIPOC and LGBTQ+[13] communities.

We do not want to imprison us as BIPOC being in a state of constant struggle, but we do think the acknowledgment of the system is the first step to our individual and collective liberation. When we know where we are starting, we can design where we are headed.

---

[13] Lesbian, Gay, Bisexual, Trans, Queer, plus Intersex, and Asexual.

Hierarchy of Needs

Many of us are familiar with Maslow's hierarchy[14] of needs as a progressive Western perspective of personal evolution and specifically self-actualization. Starting with physiological needs, safety needs, need for belongingness and love, esteem need, need to know and understand, need for aesthetics, self-actualization, and ending in transcendence. What people don't know is that Maslow spent time immersed in the Blackfoot community to study and better understand the joy experienced in this community. Although First Nations vary in community perspectives, it can be best summarized as a progression from self-actualization, community actualization, and culminating in cultural perpetuity. Meaning that self-actualization does not and could not end with the individual but rather must proceed to the community. Interesting to point out is that in the First Nations' perspective, self-actualization is inherent in the community; you begin from there.

In many ways, most BIPOC have this perspective on life (at least we have this epigenetic effect[15] in our lineages). Why does this matter in relation to Human Design? Human Design is a meta-system that is filtered through the individual and their lens; their lens is dependent on their life experience, past lives, and epigenetic cultural effects. What we see in Maslow's theories as opposed to the First

---

[14] The Blackfoot Origins of Maslow's Hierarchy of Needs (buffalosfire.com).
[15] What is epigenetics? https://www.cdc.gov/genomics/disease/epigenetics.htm#:~:text=Epigenetics%20is%20the%20study%20of,body%20reads%20a%20DNA%20sequence

Nation approach to living is that Maslow is focused on the individual and First Nation is focused on community impact.

This contrast is one that can be explained through the lens of spiral dynamics[16], a theory on human and societal development, created and evolved by Don Edward Beck and Ken Wilber and inspired by the wisdom and theories of Sri Aurobindo[17], a yoga guru, poet, philosopher, Indian nationalist and journalist, and founder of the Sri Aurobindo Ashram. In spiral dynamics there are three tiers of development, two of which are more used: The first tier is the individual development through six levels going from survival to human bond and the second tier is related to the impact on Earth and civilization. This would indicate that communities that are holistic and consider all participants, would fall into the second tier. It is also important to understand that in order for an individual or group of people to hold a certain level of development, all the preceding levels would need to be included and integrated.

---

[16] https://en.wikipedia.org/wiki/Spiral_Dynamics
[17] https://en.wikipedia.org/wiki/Sri_Aurobindo

Part 2: Origins and Systems of Culture in Human Design

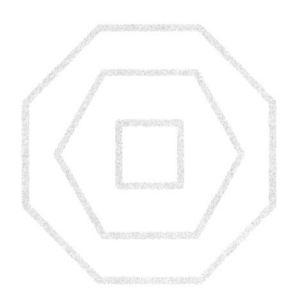

Honoring the Parts to Make the Parts Whole

Human Design is composed of the Chinese divination system, the I Ching, the Hindu chakra system, the Kabbalah, and quantum mechanics. The wholeness of these systems being mostly Indigenous systems are all a part of Human Design, and these individual parts have not been traditionally considered in the Human Design community.

People have marketed Human Design as a new complete system, cherry-picked the aspects relevant to them, and left the rest behind. The complexity of each of the parts can be overwhelming for those starting out so as a community and as teachers, we have resorted to a hierarchy of importance. This is understandable when we have so much to consider, especially as new students. However, it is important to honor the roots of this system and the people who have cultivated these teachings through thousands of years of survival in their lands of origin.

When people first find Human Design, they get education about the components of the whole system but there is not an in-depth education on why those parts are in the system and how they inform the embodiment of the chart. When we're learning about spiritual tools, it is our responsibility as spiritual teachers to investigate the origins of the systems we deem so helpful. They come from ancient cultures, and there is a benefit to deepening our understanding of them. We can utilize the hierarchy of what is most important as new students and remain curious about the parts that are actually entire living breathing systems of other cultures.

In this chapter we aim to plant the seed of the origins of tropical and sidereal astrology, the Hindu chakra system, the Jewish Kabbalah, the Chinese I Ching, and metaphysics as to help us all value the traditions that contribute to the Human Design system. In many ways, to become accomplished in each of these traditions takes decades, and all we can attempt to do as people who love Human Design is to take our time with learning, and when available, seek from these cultures. When we receive the teachings that they are grounded and rooted in, we do not lose their essence through foreign filters.

Western and Vedic Astrology

Astrology is the who, what, and where, and Human Design is the how.

—Aycee Brown

Honoring the Parts to Make the Parts Whole

Astrology is the study of stars and planets to help us understand and navigate the world and ourselves. Ancient Babylonians of Mesopotamia were among the first to chart the stars and the path of the Sun across the sky. They used a twelve-month calendar based on the phases of the Moon and using wisdom from the Sumerians before them, they established the zodiac wheel. These concepts were further refined by the Egyptians and the Greeks, and the name *zodiac* came from Greek, meaning circle of animals. The Greeks and then the Romans changed the names over the years. Astrology also spread from Mesopotamia to India, where the sidereal form[18] (Vedic) is more common. Vedic astrology has Indian spirituality and culture embedded in it.

While both Western (also known as tropical) and sidereal astrology have twelve signs, they differ in where those signs are found in the sky. The sidereal system is based on the current position of the stars, so these dates change over time as the positions of the stars move—which they do at a rate of approximately 1 degree every seventy years or so.

This is in contrast to Western astrology where the dates are fixed, and this is based on the star positions around AD 1. The two systems aligned until AD 285, when they began to diverge.

From that time, in part due to colonization, Western astrology was used mostly in the Western world. Sidereal astrology is the basis of Vedic astrology, practiced in India. In addition, sidereal astrology doesn't acknowledge the

---

[18] Reda Wigle: https://nypost.com/article/what-is-sidereal-astrology/; Sarah Regan: https://www.mindbodygreen.com/articles/vedic-astrology-101

influence of Uranus, Neptune, or Pluto in the individual's chart. It also varies in terms of what a retrograde planet means, and the relative importance of the Sun and rising signs.

Due to the constant change, sidereal astrology can be more complex and is more difficult for a novice to interpret. Western astrology is based on the tropical calendar with the four seasons, used in large parts of the world. Between tropical and sidereal there is a 24-degree difference, starting with tropical and moving clockwise toward sidereal. For instance, if your tropical Sun sign is at 0 degrees Aries, your sidereal Sun sign would be at 24 degrees Aries. It would feel logical to look at our astrological influence as an arc. As facilitators we take meta systems and bring them together, this is the way we approach astrology. Feel free to take the piece that resonates and leave the parts that don't.

We feel that both tropical and sidereal have their place in Human Design and it is how we position the way we talk about it. In the Human Design community, people pick one or the other. We see use in first having the individual look at both charts and consider the truth in each. The way we approach it is that sidereal is how we internally identify and potentially how others perceive us, and tropical is how we unfold in the world and how the Universe responds to us.

How We Consider Astrology

When it comes to Human Design, we cannot leave out our astrological composition because our natal chart influences our Human Design chart; everything has a basis in astrology, therefore our natal expression becomes a fine-tuned Human Design expression. The interconnectedness of natal astrology, centers, and gates cannot be ignored when deepening our understanding of ourselves. For instance, if you are considering your Sun in Human Design, we would recommend looking at your tropical natal chart for the astrology sign and the Human Design Gate for the hexagram, and if you want to go deeper you can do the same for sidereal.

The Hindu Chakra System

Chakras (circle or wheel), refer to the subtle body energy centers[19] which run along the length of the spine from the base of the pelvis to the top of the head. They are commonly described as the seven chakras and although more energy centers exist, these seven are the most well-known.

There is evidence of these energy centers in ancient Egypt, and Hindu traditions explore it further in the Vedas. The Vedas[20] are ancient Hindu scriptures, written in early Sanskrit contain hymns, philosophy, and guidance on rituals for priests of the Vedic religion:

> "Allied with you in your friendship, celestial immortality, the [inner] controller of the senses made the waters flow for mortals. Killed the [dormant] serpent and sent forth the Seven

---

[19] Jaram V: https://www.hinduwebsite.com/hinduism/concepts/chakras.asp; Yogesh Sharma: https://timesofindia.indiatimes.com/readersblog/my-voices/system-of-sanatan-chakra-11583/
[20] https://en.wikipedia.org/wiki/Vedas

Oceans, and opened as it were obstructed fountains." (Rig Veda IV.28.1)

In the translation, serpent, better known as kundalini (energy rising), is mentioned along with seven streams/oceans. This hymn is talking about having full control over the kundalini and subsequently awakening the seven chakras.

There are seven chakras in the human body as explained by yoga sutra and tantra texts:[21]

1. Sahasrara (सहस्रार्)
2. Agya (आज्ञा)
3. Vishuddi (विशुद्धि)
4. Anahata (अनाहत)
5. Manipura (मणिपुर)
6. Swadhisthana (स्वाधिशतान)
7. Muladhara (मूलाधार)

Kundalini Shakti (often called serpent power) is typically dormant at the base of the spine and must be awakened to reach ultimate consciousness. When kundalini awakens, it uncoils, rises, and activates the chakras to mobilize the kundalini to unite with Shiva (or consciousness) at the Agya chakra (third eye) or some believe is at Sahasrara chakra (crown). The union of Shakti and Shiva is the ultimate attainment of most yogis, giving them certain powers called

---

[21] https://www.tantra-kundalini.com/chakras/

siddhis. The *Hatha Yoga Pradipika* (foundation to yoga asana) describes the eight siddhis (Ashtasiddhi अष्टसिद्धि): [22]

- Aṇimā: reducing one's body to the size of an atom
- Mahima: expanding one's body to an infinitely large size
- Garima: becoming infinitely heavy
- Laghima: becoming almost weightless
- Prāpti: realizing whatever one desires
- Prākāmya: having unrestricted access to all places
- Iṣtva: possessing absolute lordship
- Vaśtva: the power to subjugate all

In Human Design the seven chakras create seven of the nine centers, plus we have the split of the heart chakra Anahata, which has two parts, the Higher Heart and Lower Heart, into the G Center and Will Center, and the Hindu solar plexus (Manipura) into the Spleen Center and Solar Plexus Center.

How We Consider the Chakras

In Hindu tradition, we explore each energy center more in-depth than we typically do in Human Design. In the Hindu yogic traditions, we have sound, color, structure, practices, etc. associated with each chakra. We don't approach each center separately but rather the entire system as a whole. The idea of open or definition is not one that exists in yogic terms, so for our readings we have adapted Hindu yogic

---

[22] https://nepalyogahome.com/ashta-siddhi/

and tantric practices alongside the prescriptions given in Human Design through definition/openness and through the flavors of the gates.

The Jewish Kabbalah

The image of the tree of life[23] dates far back into prehistory, with many traditions having sacred diagrams that resemble it. In the twelfth century, early Kabbalah masters in the South of France mapped the position of each of the ten interconnected Sefirah, which are arranged into seven planes and connected by thirty-two paths.

The Kabbalah Tree of Life is used in Jewish tradition to represent the manner in which consciousness (God YHWH[24]) expresses itself in creation and can be used for self-reflection. It is also used as a tool to see how and why people and events manifest in your life and can represent a practice of awareness. The connection points between the centers are derived from the map of the Kabbalah.

The Chinese I Ching

The I Ching[25] is one of the two oldest spiritual texts that has been in continuous use for over three thousand years. It is

---

[23] Lars Charles Mazzaola https://www.geneseo.edu/yoga/sefirot-tree-life; Dr. David Sanders https://kabbalahexperience.com/introduction-to-the-tree-of-life/
[24] https://en.wikipedia.org/wiki/Yahweh
[25] Associate Professor Karyn Lai: https://www.youtube.com/watch?v=Ebp2U2O9194; Dr. Geoffrey Redmond: https://www.youtube.com/watch?v=-upDG8990w8

very valued in Chinese culture. Translated, the I Ching is also known as *The Book of Changes*.

The Greeks pre-Socrates thought the world was made of one thing—that there was one element or constituent thing that existed when all matter was broken down. However, the Chinese believed the world was a plurality, and they attuned themselves to change. They believed that change was everywhere and inevitable. In addition, context is important. Identity isn't fixed but varies as you are put into different contexts, and when one thing changes, this changes the context for other things.

The oldest layers of the I Ching were supposedly composed around 1000 BC. This started off with trigrams—three lines, either broken or unbroken, which later became stacked to make hexagrams, of which there are sixty-four different permutations. The full and broken lines represent something different in the context of each hexagram.

As people have used it over the years in their spiritual practice it has been reinterpreted, and layers have been added. It was designed to provide divination on how circumstances are affecting the person who came for a reading.

There is no one author; it is collected from oral sources and includes songs, proverbs, history, etc. that were gathered together and organized around the hexagrams. It isn't a narrative designed to be read from start to finish, instead, it is divided to make it useful for divination, an oracle tool. Its use has evolved over the years. During different periods of time, the I Ching was also interpreted differently.

Your Soul Map

Each trigram has an association. Among Chinese, there are two ways of interpreting them:

1. Xiangshu–images and numbers. One uses the hexagrams primarily to calculate and use metaphysical ideas that aren't in the early texts.

2. Yili–meanings and principles. Mostly analyzes the text, and people find connections between the diagrams and the text, although there may not be a direct correlation or obvious connection.

Because this is one of the oldest texts, its ancient wisdom must be discussed, and the preservation of their transmission is vital to us. As an oracle, it has a universal language that is connected to nature and life, as well as a personal one where the individual interprets the meaning of the stories. The stories hold the transformation and guidance. They give us a direct relationship to the parts of the entire I Ching oracle system. Traditionally there are three Chinese coins that you throw to answer a question. With each coin-toss combination you decipher which six lines result in the answer given to you. This is how we arrive at an individual hexagram.

In Human Design, we have access to all the hexagrams, and depending on our definition (the parts that are colored in, giving us consistent access to its energy) in each gate, we have an opportunity to explore. First, we explore the gates that we have defined in our chart, and second, we look at how we engage with the open ones. This can be examined by how they mechanically seek to be in a state of definition, meaning that if we have an open gate and someone else has that gate defined, there is a magnetic pull toward them. We can also explore the way we experience the transits (each gate in Human Design is transited by the planets, and this creates definition) meaning if you have an open gate and the Sun is transiting that Gate, you will have an experience of definition during that transit.

In Human Design there is an evolution taking place with the hexagrams and hence the gates. There are some who prefer to maintain Ra's explanations and others who prefer to evolve the meanings. We are proposing a third option: to maintain the wisdom of the stories laid in the original I Ching and also study the synthesis of them in a one-word expression. We can both honor the stories in the I Ching for each hexagram (gate), allow the descendants of this lineage to evolve how they see fit and open up to this evolution, and utilize the one-word meaning as a starting point.

In the spirit of listening to those from the lineage, we asked Fiona Wong to comment. Since the gates play such an important role in Human Design, we felt it important to listen deeply to what Fiona has to say. What we have not conceptualized in modern culture is that ancient systems have a foundation beyond reductive information that we have about them. The I Ching is derived from a specific philosophy of life. And where we do disservice to these teachings is when we extract specifics without explaining the context. There are foundational reasons beyond gate definitions that come from this ancient philosophy. Fiona helps us understand the depth of this cultural foundation.

> "Human Design is a mechanical system. And in that, I almost envisioned this robot that's empty and

other systems can come into play here. One of the big ones is the primary health system (PHS).[26]

"There's a determination that is a cold determination. When I read about that, it was just cold foods. Well, in Chinese medicine, that doesn't work for us; it can't just be all hot or all cold. We treat things differently. For example, if there is too much dampness in the body then we treat that with some dry herbs. That's why I don't use all of Human Design at face value. And that's why I also believe there's gotta be a continuation. There's gotta be yes, the option that cold works for you—you're predisposed to that. But what if you're too cold? Or what if it's too hot, how do we lower the body temperature safely?

"In Chinese medicine, we also have meridians. So I know in Human Design, we say that certain centers are related to certain organs. We have a very similar system in Chinese medicine that doesn't necessarily match up to Human Design. So, for me, as a Chinese American—which system am I using? I will always default to Chinese medicine because I grew up in it and it works for me. I don't even use the PHS with a lot of my clients because I feel it's very incomplete. I have a mentor who was around Human Design in the beginning, and he always tells me -this wasn't around in the beginning, this wasn't there. This was added later on. So, for me, I don't

---

[26] PHS: Primary Health System: a secondary branch of Human Design that was added later by Ra.

know whether it was a cash grab from Ra when that system came about or whether there's something to it. But to me, it feels so incomplete that when people ask me about PHS, I say, let's bring in a Chinese medicine practitioner. If you really want to dive into that, let's move into a different system—a sister system." (Fiona Wong, pers. comm.)

How Fiona Approaches the I Ching

"So, growing up, in my culture, everyone divines. I don't want to say it's not special—it's just that it's intertwined in our culture. Every woman I knew could read faces, read palms, read all of these things.

"So, like some of the I Ching—it's just in daily life, but it's something that you meditate on. One of my favorite gates is my North Node, Gate 60—limitation. And for me, I don't even really touch upon nodes and gates, unless I've been doing readings for a specific person for a while, because I don't see it as something that is fixed in your chart.

"I see it as a flavor that constantly changes throughout your life. So, for me, I see Gate 60—limitation. I feel limited by my mental health. I feel limited by the fact that I don't have a defined Sacral, but that limitation is a constant question of—and what else is there? If we cannot break through this door because of said limitation, can we take a step back and see if there are other doors there?

"And that is a daily meditation for me. It's a—what other doors are there? Every time I hit a roadblock, what other doors are there? Or do I need to step back? If someone comes up to me saying, 'I'm working on understanding my G Center and how identity works,' then you have Gate 1 active in there that can just open up the conversation to so many questions.

"Instead of sitting there and (saying) Gate 1 means this, and that means you have to act like this and pigeonhole yourself; instead, do this characteristic, and it becomes a meditation practice. I feel like that's how it was initially meant to be, you know, you throw the sticks, you read the changing lines and you don't get an instruction manual that says you need to do this, you get something that you meditate upon. You get something that opens up your awareness.

"And I feel like that's how Human Design in an ideal world should be used. We shouldn't be forcing ourselves to act differently. It should open your awareness. I do like the analogy of watching yourself as a movie, where I'm aware of this. So is this something that I want to keep in my life? Is this something I want to shift? And I feel like I Ching can do a lot for that." (Fiona Wong, pers. comm.)

Fiona Expands on Human Design Interpretation, the I Ching, and Patriarchy

"I don't remember whether it was Richard Rudd or Ra but one of them said the I Ching was very misogynistic and in Human Design, they're hoping to correct some of that.

> "And it felt very 'white savior' to me. I was just like—yeah, we have our problems, but we will fix it internally, and we're working on it internally. We don't need someone to come in and rewrite our history or our story. If there are misogynistic or problematic things in the I Ching, we will address that, and that is something for us to evolve and grow into. And that's not even limited to people who are Chinese, but the students of it, and people who have been a part of the system. That's something to tackle." (Fiona Wong, pers. comm.)

The Incarnation Cross

The Incarnation Cross is the sum of the gates of the conscious/unconscious Sun and Earth in your Human Design body graph. The Incarnation Cross is also a big marker of how we unfold in the world and what we attract to us. We ask Fiona's view on it.

> "I do enjoy the Incarnation Cross because in my culture, we believe in reincarnation and that is something that I'm very clear about. It doesn't matter what background or religion my client comes from. I do bring my belief systems to the table, and you can take whatever interpretation you need from that. In my culture, we believe that there's a reason why we are incarnated into this lifetime.

"And I really enjoy using Human Design, especially the four-quarters[27], to help people understand what that is. 'Cause I feel like a lot of us ask that big question. What's my life's purpose? What am I here to do? And it's frustrating for some clients when I tell them 'You're not necessarily here to do anything, but there is an energy, a spirit that you are embodying, a force that you are bringing forward in this lifetime, and your Incarnation Cross can't tell you what exactly it will be, but it will tell you how you are predisposed to enter certain situations.'

"As Projectors, we feel like we're a lot sometimes because we have that penetrating energy. Let's say my client is someone who is in a relationship with the man of the house, and they feel like they don't have a voice. You can use their Incarnation Cross or even the I Ching—when we bring in some of the flavor text, you can use that as a prompt to ask, 'Where does this come from?' Now we're talking about trauma. Why do you feel like you might be in this situation? Is there a cultural thing that told you that this is a woman's worth, this is what you should be doing?

"We can use the pieces of Human Design to ask them questions such as knowing your Incarnation Cross, do you believe that there's another route you might want to take? Do you believe there are other doors out there available to you? And we can

---

[27] All hexagrams are arranged in a wheel or circle in Human Design; this wheel is divided into four parts: quarters; the Initiation, Civilization, Duality, and Mutation.

use the Incarnation Cross and I Ching—all of these things, to support where they want to head next." (Fiona Wong, pers. comm.)

The Evolution of Human Design Language and I Ching

The sixty-four individual hexagrams in the I Ching are equivalent to the sixty-four gates in the Human Design system.

> "I think all practitioners should write their own personal gates. I call it a commonplace book and I tell all my students to do it, so when you read something about Human Design, when you have some sort of revelation or a different understanding, especially based on your own life experience, put it down. Because I'm not supposed to interpret Gate 1 the same way someone else does, because it's impossible. We have completely different life experiences and journeys.

> "So when you experience something or you feel some sort of activation, put it down, whether it's in Evernote or on a piece of paper, and come up with your own commonplace book for it. There is no other way to learn this stuff than to be in the story, to experience the story, and document your own understanding.

> "It's not about being right or wrong in that sense, I feel like the only true, correct way to use the I Ching system is to live your life and be reflective, because that's what it's for. It's just a giant book of journal prompts, really.

"There's literally no rule in the I Ching system saying that we can't rename it [the gates]. It's so flexible. It's supposed to be for each individual person. I would even say it's the original Human Design. It's for you to use however you want to use it. You can't start strong-arming other people to use it that way too–that's where we're getting patriarchal. We're getting oppressive when we force other people to see it our way. So I really hope everyone can kind of come to the understanding that this is not really a system to be saying this is how it is and that's it 'cause Ra or whoever said so." (Fiona Wong, pers. comm.)

Metaphysics

Quantum mechanics is the branch of physics that deals with the behavior of particles–atoms, electrons, and photons–in the molecular and sub-molecular realm. Many of the principles in quantum mechanics are counter to those in traditional physics, as particles tend to behave differently at that level.

At the quantum level, when you investigate the particles that make up the atom, you will see that atoms have no physical structure, and instead are made up of energy. This is an important concept in quantum mechanics[28], the idea

---

[28] Adam Mann, Robert Coolman: https://www.livescience.com/33816-quantum-mechanics-explanation.html; Valeria Sabater: https://exploringyourmind.com/the-dalai-lama-on-quantum-physics-and-spirituality/

that we are all made up of energy—and that in fact everything is made up of energy.

One of the most fundamental and important pieces in the mystery of a soul having a human experience actually boils down to math and science. *As above, so below.* This Hermetic[29] principle has its origins in Egypt.

The Kemetic people believed that the heavens and Earth were governed by the same principle (Ma'at). "As above, so below" is written on Kemetic tombs from the Predynastic period[30].

Science tells us that the creation of our planet is due to the big bang, and the Kemetic principle above would suggest that this same quantum collapsing occurs inside of us; in fact, the creation of life is a single event of the egg and sperm merging. Life on Earth is an evolutionary process and as it continues, we are tasked to ensure the evolution is toward the direction we envision for generations to come.

Math and science are challenging to understand, and it is our job to clean our bodies and reduce inflammation in our brains so that we can understand the ancient wisdom of receiving biochemical information from Sun-centric information. Sunrise gives our brain and body activation of hormone response, and at sunset we receive production of melatonin, but we have separated ourselves from these cycles with artificial light and an overabundance of food and comfort.

---

[29] https://en.wikipedia.org/wiki/Hermeticism
[30] https://futiledemocracy.wordpress.com/2011/07/26/as-above-so-below/

Your Soul Map

In *Your Spark Is Light*, Dr. Courtney Hunt explains how quantum physics seems to be bridging philosophy and science. She mentions Dr. Michio Kaku and his definition of consciousness: "consciousness is all the feedback loops necessary to create a model of yourself in space, in relationship to others, and in time, especially forward in time." Dr. Hunt states "in order to evolve we have to receive signals from our environment, specifically from light via electron excitation of DHA in the retina… this is what allowed us to develop larger brains, the ability to make ATP or energy in our mitochondria, and in turn the capability of memory storage or perception of time."[31]

She further states and quotes Sir Roger Penrose, a mathematical physicist and philosopher: "In order for us to understand consciousness, we have to understand physics."[32]

The take-home message is that we have more power than we realize. We have been kept from the knowledge but have also chosen to remove ourselves from the knowledge.

The neutrino stream (subatomic particles that run through our bodies) is constantly affecting us, and even Ra speaks of it in *The Human Design Book* (The Black Book). In this book he states "Black holes are considered the birthing ground of stars and galaxies. When these objects are struck by a strong enough force, the impact releases unimaginable energy and matter which eventually coalesce into stars. Our own Sun's solar system was born out of such

---

[31] https://www.courtneyhuntmd.com/your-spark-is-light
[32] Suojanen M. Conscious experience and quantum consciousness theory: Theories, causation, and identity. E-LOGO. 2019; 26(2): 14-34. Doi: 10.18267/j.e-logos.465

an event. According to relativity, time began with the birth of the universe. According to the mystics, creation took place in a time before the universe. The Human Design System is based on seeing relativity as relative. Just as Newton's laws are relative to Earth, so too Einstein's theory is relative to the universe after the big bang." (2011, 3)

Karen Curry Parker says "In the story of Human Design, when the body is upright and the Head Center is pointing upward, the chart gets activated by the neutrino stream, which is from the side. So that's why there's that solar or heliophilic orientation around the Sun."

To us, this speaks of the potentiality of each creation and the science that unfolds in every moment.

The Human Design chart is the synthesis of who we are, but we have to be willing to do the work to uncover it. The chart is the easiest, most accessible doorway for us to tap into the infinite possibilities available to all of us; we all have access to the full chart. When we clean our bodies and our brains, we will be able to fully access the entire system. For now, by leaning into astrology and Human Design charts we have a roadmap to arrive at the space where we actualize our liberation. At the moment of this liberation, the chart in many ways becomes secondary. We do not need to do this overnight but rather we can compassionately decondition our bodies and brains and begin to slowly tap into our vitality and our communication with the intelligence in the galaxies.

The Chakras and Our Evolution

According to Human Design, the chakra system has made changes. The first change was in 1782 from a seven center (traditional Hindu chakra system) to a split of the heart chakra (into the G Center and the Will Center), and the solar plexus chakra (into Spleen and Solar Plexus Centers). In 2027, the Solar Plexus Center will mutate.

Karen Curry Parker has a unique and important role regarding this subject, because she was a direct student of Ra. She offers a first-hand explanation to the evolution of humanity.

> "I think we have to look at this first mutation in 1782 and know it is not complete; it's just staging for 2027. There's so much I could say about this, so I'm going to do my best to keep it succinct.

> "So, the way that I would explain it is that first of all consciousness shifts, and then the chart shifts, not the other way around. And I think that's a really important thing to understand because we're all like, 'When is 2027 going to get here?' and yet we're in it. It's going to happen after we're done. We're already doing the work of 2027.

> "So preceding the split in 1782, we had a scientific revolution which actually ended with the end of Newton's life, which was before the split. In the scientific revolution, we sought to codify the material world in an attempt to establish a pathway to sovereignty.

> "If you think about how the world was before the scientific revolution, you couldn't wake up one

morning as a stable boy and say, 'I'm just going to set my sights on being the king. I'm going to visualize it. I'm going to see it and know what it's like.' That wasn't a thing—you were what you were. And to a certain degree, your pathway was going to be largely determined by either you being subject to some ruler, king, or emperor, or you being a subject to the church, especially in the Western world. Now I will say, and this is a really important thing to know, I don't know a lot about the history of say Africa or Asia at that time, although I'm going to suspect, at least in Asian history, there were emperors and rulers too, and there wasn't a whole lot of personal sovereignty. I don't know what it was like in other areas of the world at that time. So please know that this is a very Western European perspective, and the scientific revolution is to a certain degree, still a Western phenomenon.

"So, what happened was, as we learned to codify and look at the function of the material world, we had the emergence of reasoning and logic and scientific methodology. As we began to be able to codify and systematize our understanding of the world, it started to make us think of ourselves as living biological creatures, as being capable of following a formula, and so we began to organize society in a formulaic way. We started to build things like school systems, government systems, and healthcare systems. The Industrial Revolution happened, and we started to create things in a systematized model. We had corporations and we had a whole change in the way in which society organized itself at that point.

"And one of the new ideas that emerged was the idea that you had sovereignty over your life. For example, some people could choose who they were going to marry. That was truer for men than it was for women and certainly for white Western men than for anybody else, but they started to have a little bit more choice over their lot in life.

"So, individuation is really what the Will Center is about; the Will Center is the personal self that is designed to be of service to others, and we'll use Traditional Human Design language here, your collective, or your higher self, or your higher purpose, which is the G Center.

"The G Center contains the potential of the higher expression of the human story, and we program what we allow ourselves to receive through the Monopole by the quality of the value that we place on our own personal identity—the unique, vital expression of who we are in this incarnation.

"The Magnetic Monopole resides in our G Center; it is the driver for the direction and trajectory of our life. It is a magnet that only attracts and does not repel and contains the unconscious genetic Design [the red gates in the chart] and conscious genetic Personality [the black gates in the chart][33]." (Karen Curry Parker, pers. comm.)

_____

[33] https://www.geneticmatrix.com/the-magnetic-monopole/

The Solar Plexus Chakra Split and Quantum Creativity

"There are two parts of the story. First it is setting us up for where we're headed. The second part is the solar plexus chakras. Because prior to the solar plexus chakra split, we were purely instinctual beings. We were reactive and motivated or driven by fear and survival. With this split and the emergence of the Emotional Solar Plexus, we now see the beginning of the potential for deliberate creation—for creation or being able to create by virtue of frequencies.

"And that is quantum creativity. That's the next piece where now you are able to, if you know how, consciously and deliberately hold a specific frequency of emotional energy. This in turn calibrates the heart into a state of coherence or incoherence, depending on what kind of frequency you're holding, and it also programs the Monopole and then starts to attract into your life things that match the quality of the frequency you are holding.

"So the heart chakra split; the solar plexus chakra split. It's training wheels. We're not there yet, but we've been exploring—how do we create in this new way?

"The problem is, I think, dual fold. The first problem is, we have a crisis, and I think we haven't figured it out yet. The Will Center is in a crisis of value. And part of why the Will Center is operating from a crisis place is that we haven't healed the trauma. We haven't healed collective trauma, and collective trauma—or trauma in general—is stored in Gate 26, the Gate of Integrity in Human Design or the Gate of The Trickster–that's what Ra called it–which is the shadow of that gate, because the high expression of that gate is the alignment of self-worth and value.

"We are still trying to figure out 'what is value, what is my value'–but we haven't figured that out Gate 55, which is where abundance lives, yet it's also the frequency that regulates our enoughness and sufficiency. If I'm having a crisis in my value, I can't have faith, I am buying into lack-consciousness, because if I am not enough, then I can't believe in enoughness.

"And this is sort of the big thing we've been playing with through the current collective transit of the Cross of Planning [comprising Gates 37, 40, 9, 16] moving into the Cross of The Sleeping Phoenix [comprising Gates 55, 59, 20, 34]. We move from Gate 37 being the driver to having Gate 55 be the driver, and also the Solar Plexus driver or the driver for value. The Cross of Planning is initiated by Gate 37 which is the Gate of Friendship, and the Cross of The Sleeping Phoenix is initiated by Gate 55 which is abundance in spirit. The driver evolves from relationships to connection to Spirit." (Karen Curry Parker, pers. comm.)

The 2027 Evolution

"Here's the thing–our charts are not going to change, but our consciousness is changing, and the chart itself as the next generation that begins to emerge in 2027, who has the new Design, they're already going to be collectively conditioned, hopefully, by the shifts that we've been working on for fifty years.

"I think 2027 will be a big bang moment. When we have new discoveries in science, those are also artifacts of shifts in consciousness. We can't manifest an idea on the planet if consciousness doesn't precede it.

"In the late 1800s, quantum scientists were looking at quantum particles and going, holy moly—these things don't act like matter at all: they show up in the way we expect them to show up. And if I expect it to be over here and you expect to be over there, it shows up in both places. How is that a thing?

"All of a sudden, we start to really have active conversations in science and in philosophy and religion in some cases, or at least spirituality around how our perceptions and our expectations influence outcomes. That was a really big idea. And so now we see not only quantum physics as beginning to be recognized as an actual body of science, but we also see, growing up along with it, the New Thought movement.

"We start to see Madame Blavatsky, Rudolf Steiner, Ernest Holmes and The Science of Mind, Unity Consciousness, and Charles and Myrtle Fillmore. Napoleon Hill comes out with a book called *Think and Grow Rich*. Suddenly mindset and energy, Florence Scovel Shinn, all of these people started having the same idea around the same time—it's the energy first, then the action. And we're still really in baby steps with this, but that's what we're moving toward with the Solar Plexus mutation.

"If you look at the Cross of The Sleeping Phoenix, it says when you are living in the embodiment of enoughness, you have the faith to know that you can create, in response, everything that everyone needs. You can unify people around common ideas and convictions that provide sustainable support for everyone. That's what we're headed to. The 2027 story came through The Voice, it was part of the very original reception from Ra.

"And I'm looking at the Solar Plexus mutation going, how the hell did you get that interpretation out of the Cross of The Sleeping Phoenix? That is the ultimate extreme shadow of the Cross of The Sleeping Phoenix. You have the sustainability center, the Sacral Center, that is all about what I need to do to love people, to take care of people.

"And I'm thinking, he didn't have a defined Sacral. He had no idea what it meant to have a Sacral. So, he's talking about this dystopian 'pure freak future' (his words) where everybody's just this radical individual gunning people down.

"He walked away from his kids. I'm sorry, you [Ra] don't have defense circuitry[34]. I'm not saying that that's an open/defined Sacral thing. But I think that to a certain degree the energy resources for

---

[34] Defense circuit is one of the Human Design circuits that relates to primal energy; how to provide and nourish others.

sustainable caring weren't there because he probably didn't learn it.

"And second, he burned it out. If you reframe it and you look at the high expression of the Sacral, the Cross of The Sleeping Phoenix says, no, that's not our future. Our future is that we're going to build sustainably. We're really responding to the needs of the people and everybody's going to have enough.

"But I will say, I think there's some merit to listening to the shadow of this because I do think that if you look at the system theories, and you look at any time you go up an ascension curve in a system theory, before you go up that ascension curve, when the system shifts, you have dynamic instability. The static stability hits dynamic instability, and it starts to move around and gets disrupted, and out of that disruption comes an ascension curve.

"I do think that where we are—and this is why I think Human Design actually showed up on the planet at this time—is at a point in that dynamic instability where we're still going to get to the good part. But the question now is, how are we going to get there? Are we going to take this path where we are saying, 'Timeout, no more guns, this is stupid; we are not going to live on a planet where we do this to our children or to each other!?'

"And how are we going to create that? And of course, the way we have to create it—as much as everybody hates this on Facebook right now—the very first thing we have to do is (a) clear our own trauma so we're not reacting, but we're being deliberate, which is really the purpose of the Solar Plexus Center, and (b) we have to hold the energy for the possibility because we don't know how, but the how will get delivered if we keep building the energetic scaffolding. So, thoughts and prayers are actually important.

"In fact, if you go back to the Institute of HeartMath®, we know that thoughts and prayers can actually shift the geomagnetic environment. And so you have to also think that maybe that's shifting the neutrino stream and how the neutrino stream gets delivered, and how the Monopoles are being programmed and how the conditioning field for the not-born-yet people on the planet are being conditioned in the Design Crystals[35] that are waiting for the next souls to snatch them up.

"Or do we go the death of the material route? And that's where we keep pushing. We keep shooting, we keep bombing, we keep whatever. And then we have to get to the point where enough of us are like, this is dumb. We're not doing this anymore. And then we can create what we want to create.

---

[35] The Design Crystal sits at the Ajna and is the force that operates and maintains the body. The Personality Crystal sits at the Head Center and is the energy that represents who we think we are. The Design is the vehicle, the Magnetic Monopole is the Driver, and the Personality Crystal is the Passenger. https://www.jovianarchive.com/Stories/10/Introduction_to_the_Human_Design_System

"We're at a crossroads in terms of how we're going to get there." (Karen Curry Parker, pers. comm.)

The Frequency of Gate 55

The Gate of Faith[36], Gate 55, will be the frequency of energy throughout the next global cycle, starting with the Solar Plexus mutation in 2027.

> "It initiates in the 55—Sun and the 55. So, the Earth itself has global cycles. They are about 400 years long and we are in the global cycle Cross of Planning. And what happens on February 22nd, 2027, is we shift into a new global cycle and that new global cycle is ruled by the Incarnation Cross of The Sleeping Phoenix.
>
> "In the new Solar Plexus chart, the hard wiring in the channels shifts, and the way the energy moves in the channels also shifts. Part of what happens is the [Channel] 19/49 comes apart, which means our relationship with nature and the way in which we eat changes, which is already happening.
>
> "In the 19/49, at the moment, in its connection, we needed to eat mammals, because it grounded us. With that need gone, now we don't have to eat meat anymore. We can be vegan and it's not going to unground us. And our way of consuming the resources of the planet is changing and our ability to digest and the way in which we process food changes, plus our relationship with nature itself

---

[36] Quantum Human Design™ language was created by Karen Curry Parker and is used throughout her interview.

changes. So that piece comes apart. The 55 becomes the driver with the Sun and the 55. The 50/27 moves over, and it moves into the ego circuit and into the business part of the ego circuit. So it's now connected to the 54/32, the 50/27, the 44/26, and the 45/21. So business becomes responsible.

"It becomes responsible business. The flow of the energy in the channels changes. The channels still exist; it's just that 19/49 comes apart. The 50/27 gets added to the ego circuit. And then the flow of energy goes from the 55 to the 39, up to the 36 and over to the 59/6." (Karen Curry Parker, pers. comm.)

We don't necessarily agree that everyone will feel called to be vegan; this is a personal choice. Due to our ancestral lineage, some of us are not intended to be vegan. The point is to look at how we regard our food supply with more consciousness.

Among the Profile Types, the designation of the Projector emerged around the same time of the 1st split and the role of Projectors has a special importance as noted by Karen Curry Parker:

"The other thing is the Projector is a new Type that emerged in 1782. It is the role of the Projector to hold the template of possibility in place on an energetic level, so that when they're looking at the world, they're like, Oh, this needs to move in, this needs to move, and you need to do this, you need to know this, because they are basically holding that entire infrastructure for what's to come, in place. And it's exhausting, that's why Projectors are really tired.

"I have a Projector, a thirteen-year-old, and she tells me she has a very deep and intimate relationship with dragons and the dragons live in the fifth dimension. Now I'm really careful with my kids. (I don't teach them anything that I do because I really want them to discover it for themselves. I want them to have the opportunity to have a normal life.) She tells me all the time, that the dragons are going to come back, and that everybody has a dragon bond. The role of the dragons is to build a bridge between the fifth dimension and the third dimension.

"And the other day she pops out. I'm like, *'Tell me, what is this fifth dimension?'* She goes, *'Well, mom, it's the field of emotional energy obviously.'* And I'm thinking, *'This is creeping me out because this is the Solar Plexus mutation.'* Whether it's dragons or not, intuitively as a Projector, she knows—the emotional body of the planet is essential to the evolution of humanity and that piece has to get regulated.

"The other thing that happens in the Solar Plexus mutation, and why it's called the Solar Plexus mutation, is that the waves of the Solar Plexus get fixed—not fixed as in broken but fixed as in—they get stabilized. And so, all of this volatility that we have right now gets stabilized. Which is why I think this whole gunning people down in combat thing doesn't make sense. That's an emotional thing. I don't think we know what it's going to be like, but I don't think we're going to be reactive in the way that we are right now, because that whole wave of lack and abundance isn't happening.

"I think that the explanation is—what's the world going to be like when we don't have lack as a ruling force and we're not pushing against contrast to create something better, when we're already in that sufficiency? And then what are we going to create? And I really do think we're on the cusp of a massive creative revolution and we're just still locked in our conditioning, thinking, *Oh, it's going to be hard.*

"If you look at the wiring of a Will Center, it is almost a hundred percent Tribal circuitry[37], except for the 25/51, which is the Channel of The Priestess or The Shaman that reminds us if we get too far off course, we get shocked back into the fulfillment of our true and higher purpose.

"And the true and higher purpose means we occupy our value so that we create sustainable value, and we can share who we are and the value we create with the world. We're designed to share, and it's the shadow of ego and the not-enoughness of the shadow of ego that's caused us to lose connection with our collective identity." (Karen Curry Parker, pers. comm.)

Because we are experiencing a planetary and collective change and given that Human Design is a living breathing system, there is an opportunity to evolve the lens and the application in these changing times. The pervasive lens has

---

[37] The tribal or community circuitry focuses on family, friends, and community.

been one-dimensional only considering human experiences as all the same and not considering the lived nuanced reality of people of color. As the new lens develops, the inclusion of BIPOC personal stories and space to evolve the Human Design language grows, creating a more inclusive and equitable system for accessing the soul's intelligence.

How to Trust Human Design in an Unsafe World

Just as some of us trust the Bible, it is imperative for us to open ourselves up to spiritual tools and texts that can provide us the freedom to explore our own truth and destiny. Because we're not always attuned with our soul-makings and our ancestral path, it is harder for us to embrace concepts that have been taken away from us or that we have not been given access to. Human Design allows us to take back our power and set the rules for our own lives. It is a portal to the self and provides access to the inner workings of our soul intelligence. There's an understanding that a system was created by someone with power and privilege who did not see the BIPOC experience, but we cannot disregard the magic that the parts hold when combined into the Human Design system. If we can set aside the founder's ethics and practices and look at the information translated *through* him, then we can embrace how the system can help us.

We want to be clear: *who* transmits the system matters. As leaders and people with influence, we have to learn to hold our responsibility of being guides as important, but we cannot control the nature of the conduits of important information. Please understand that we are at great tension with sounding as if we are condoning any harm so that we can access Human Design. *We Are Not.* The honest thing is that we have both benefited from using Human Design immensely and we take on the responsibility of being teachers in this space, to bring more ethics and to decondition the language and approach to the system. We understand that the origins of how and when it was created do not sit well with many, but we cannot disregard its effectiveness.

Honoring Your Lived Experience

This or any other system does not take away from what we, as BIPOC, have gone through in this world. What Human Design *can* do is bring clarity to these lived experiences and help us understand how to navigate going forward. The reason we have put these writings together is to create safety in our individual and collective experiences and provide a space where as BIPOC we do not have to translate or filter unconscious bypassing spiritual concepts. Our lived experience is valid, and we also know that within each of us is potential beyond the expectations set by our society and even our well-meaning family.

The Agency of Your Life

Even when we feel depleted and deflated by the world, our contribution and effort matter. As a community, we have to continue to choose our vitality and liberation day after day. Although some days it may feel exhausting, we have to remember to rest and to know deep in our bones that sweetness and richness are available to us, that joy is available to us, and that living a life that allows us access and abundance is our birthright. We have agency in our lives and seeking a community that believes this for us, with us, and for each of us, strengthens us all. There is power in invoking ancestral cultures living deep in our DNA that focus on community, and the strength and power in the whole to support the individual. We are not alone in this. Part of the colonization program is to extract us from our truth, from our traditional practices, and from the way of life that has given us clarity and direction for centuries. In this dawn of the Aquarian era[38], it is time to take this anointing for ourselves and for the good of all. We are an important piece of the puzzle of the evolution of our civilization.

Creating Safe Spaces Within Spiritual Modalities

Non-BIPOC in spiritual spaces generally have a perspective of seeing the potential of BIPOC, and as BIPOC, we feel that they see us for that potential and want to get to know us and acknowledge us. Yet deep down they sense that we are more powerful because of our direct ancestral access to these spiritual teachings. As a result, it's easier for non-BIPOC to ignore us or not include us. As cultures, whiteness

---

[38] https://www.wellandgood.com/what-is-age-aquarius/

chose a path of colonizing, and although pagan traditions were abolished and people were forced to subjugate, as a whole, the division of skin color positioned one group over another.

It's hard to quantify what will make spiritual spaces safer for BIPOC. However, there first needs to be an acknowledgment that we aren't prominent in these spaces at all. That is part of the problem, and the solution lies in shifting this reality. As BIPOC we cannot invalidate our lived experience and it is also important to not stay in our narratives of the past but rather move toward empowerment and the belief that we are intended to be whole and abundant. Again, community support matters. Let's bring more awareness of who we learn from and who we are influenced by.

Whose books are we reading? We understand that non-BIPOC are more prevalent in the publishing and spiritual industries and yet we have to also remember the power of voting with our dollar. Let's start by supporting BIPOC-driven spiritual initiatives and inviting spiritual teachers and influencers to sit in those spaces, ensuring that they are compensated for their time and wisdom. The answer to this question of safety is complex and this simple act of investing in BIPOC wisdom is an amazing start that can ripple into unimaginable well-being.

Finding Joy

Black joy is nuanced and layered. We are NOW more open to seeking it; however, there is an underlying subconscious layer of worry that we hold and carry in our bodies. For instance, there is the TikTok "Black men frolicking"[39] movement where Black men film themselves running through fields, and there was a comment by a white man about how these videos made him pause because he realized that Black men have to select fields that are safe for them.

Privilege and Its Influence

At one point Human Design was inaccessible to BIPOC individuals due to costs, and most spiritual modalities that become popular carry an undertone that it is "for non-BIPOC" due to the pricing barriers alone. Social barriers within the spiritual community are also limiting because many spaces have only one Black or one Brown person making it a guarded space to learn or share in. Unless people have trauma (i.e., growing up LGBTQ+) or are neurodivergent, non-BIPOC rarely have to consider safety as a barrier. There is also privilege in embodying a spiritual modality, as non-BIPOC do not have the same trauma or view of the world. Although non-BIPOC women feel the "witch wound" and it is valid, the level of suppression of spirituality in BIPOC is of greater magnitude.

Power Dynamics and Access

When we are in positions of authority it is essential to understand the power dynamic in spaces and to also be clear that there is a system of oppression running through

---

[39] https://www.yahoo.com/video/black-men-frolicking-bringing-much-173238742.html

our programming. We have to be mindful that as leaders we hold the unconscious power and that others are impacted by this. For example, if a student or client expresses a concern, we have to have a process in place to have repair conversations, especially if they hold an identity within a marginalized group.

Part 3: Integration and Equity of Human Design

Meeting Yourself with a New Lens

Human Design in its current state has been positioned for one view and experience; there has not been much room for nuance and acknowledgment of a system of oppression that is very real for those of us who experience its effects.

Realities of Human Design Aura Types

There is a generational attitude that pervaded from 1970-2000 where *liberation* of the individual lay in the hands and mindset of such individuals. This means that we were fed that to be liberated, to be abundant, to be in bliss on this material plane meant we controlled our psyche to move from *victim to victorious*. Anything less than empowerment meant we were not fully doing our inner work, or as we say in Human Design, our deconditioning work, which became during this time the gatekeeping aspect of keeping BIPOC unaware of tools and systems that could help the journey of the victim to victorious path. So, when we look at Aura Types from this perspective it is tough for us to grasp these perspectives fully because it is tough for us to place ourselves in the validity of it. The concern we hear often is people questioning why we have not heard or been invited into hearing about it.

There was a surge of millennial white women who realized Human Design was not as well-known and capitalized on the novelty of the system. In many ways, it was a wake-up call for those of us who have utilized this system to begin to share the mystery of it. For those of us who are stewards of this knowledge and wisdom, we are having to reposition the lens of whiteness in Human Design interpretations to retrofit our BIPOC experience. This retrofit is not just about our pain, but also our incredible and unique access to joy.

Why It Looks Different for Us

When we categorize Human Design Profiles from a BIPOC experience, the traditional approach becomes insufficient. Since our society is changing, and the outdated category of *Generators are worker bees* no longer fits as we realize the influence colonization and capitalism have in our day-to-day as a society. We need to re-conceptualize what initiation, leadership, work, mutation, evolution, and well-being looks like, especially for BIPOC. As we do this work, it is inevitable that blind spots will develop and creating an approach that addresses those spaces will be important to the evolution of the Human Design system.

Human Design Through a Critical Lens

In order to understand our blind spots as a community, we have to listen to those who the system is not working for, primarily those most marginalized in society and those whose voices are rarely heard in spiritual circles. Elmina Bell is a neurodivergent expansive person[40] who has a Black liberation lens and Black psychology education. She came to Human Design with the hope of getting further insight into herself, but she had a reading that felt unfinished and lacking in acknowledging her lived experience. From our perspective it seems as though the language used in this reading was evidence of an incomplete, whitewashed approach to the Human Design system. Because we are interested in the critique of this system, we wanted to deeply listen to her perspective as an outsider, yet someone who holds a critical lens and who is also an astrologer. We find that many BIPOC want to come to the system and experience it in its entirety but because of the origins and language, BIPOC individuals find it challenging to fully accept the system that could benefit them and, due to the barriers, give up on exploring it.

The unintended effect of the lack of an equity lens in Human Design has led many to have experiences and readings that leave the client unsettled. We specifically interviewed Elmina, as she brings a critical lens to the origins of Human Design and has extensive experience with astrology. We do not want to sugarcoat some of the problematic pieces of the communal Human Design narrative. We believe that we

---

[40] https://medium.com/@ngwagwa/neuroexpansive-thoughts-9db1e566d361

can both be critical, rectify any harm being done, and use the system to help us all be our authentic liberated selves. Elmina's experience is not an isolated instance, and it is a reminder of the great responsibility we have to be stewards of this system, especially as we spread the message of Human Design to all kinds of people.

Whatever feelings rise up as you read, please consider the unique privilege of listening to a Black neurodivergent human who has an academic, work, and lived experience in Black liberation and decolonizing arenas. This is our collective opportunity to listen and learn.

> "The thing is, in all the different jobs and the different places I was in—like the theater or political science, which I used to do, now I'm in mental health and spirituality—the reason why I was there wasn't changing. I was using whatever I was doing to help liberate Black people. With the theater, we were not doing Shakespeare. We were doing Black plays to tell Black people's stories. Then when I went to political science, we were looking at laws and things that keep Black people from advancing. Then with mental health, we were looking at African understandings of mental health, and we were learning about the eugenics[41] that is in psychology.
>
> "The language of Human Design makes it more susceptible to eugenics than other spiritual and religious practices because of the hierarchy and

---

[41] Eugenics: the study of how to arrange reproduction within a human population to increase the occurrence of heritable characteristics regarded as desirable. https://www.britannica.com/science/eugenics-genetics

because of the use of the word undefined, and because of the way things are instantly labeled good or bad. If you don't have the [psychology] background—specifically Black psychology—which, unless you went to an HBCU [Historically Black College or University] to get your psych degree, you probably wouldn't be able to spot it because they're not teaching that in the regular psych classes. They aren't teaching how energy is categorized and how people's thinking processes or existing processes are labeled. We're not really taught in Western psych programs, the history of psychology, and how eugenic it was, and even Western medicine and biology are rooted in anti-Blackness and anti-Indigeneity. In all of these things where they are using white people's culture as the measuring stick and as the standard of what is a good thing versus what is a bad thing.

"So, I think a lot of the switching around Human Design is like getting out of these mindsets of listing something as lacking, i.e., Oh, you don't have this, this is undefined or this is open, so it's bad. Just say what it is, instead of attaching all of these labels and these over-categorizations, that's what confuses people.

"I feel that it is important for me to name that I am defined by Indigenous African modalities, Abolition, and Healing Justice Praxis, so I just don't feel like Human Design, a privileged white man's invention, created through cultural appropriation has enough range to truly help me. Additionally, the Human Design founder disrespects the Indigenous peoples who cultivated the spiritual systems he appropriated by conveniently extracting some parts from them and mixing them up rather than centering their foundations in the system. This erases the sacredness and depth of those cultures. I also want to name that I don't think Human Design can be decolonized because it was created by a white person through the colonial means of cultural appropriation. Decolonization is about removing colonial mentalities from spaces already existing prior to colonization/white dominance. For instance, medicine, psychology, or agriculture can be decolonized. But Human Design didn't exist before colonization and was created through appropriative means, but Human Design readers can improve their spiritual practices by directly studying the traditions the Human Design founder Ra appropriated from.

"Something I would have also liked to see, because I had heard from people who do Human Design and had read online, is that it is connected to, or originates from, these other traditions, like the Kabbalah, the I Ching, and stuff like that, and I would have liked to see that coming through in my reading. And again, I know that not all Human Design readers are the same.

"Maybe there are Human Design readers that are already doing this, but I can only speak to my reading that I got from the person who did it. I didn't learn anything about I Ching Proverbs or I didn't even know what my I Ching connection was. So if somebody could bring in–'your Gate is 54' because the different numbers are supposed to be representing different in I Ching. If they could have shown me what my I Ching Proverbs were, I could feel more connected to the culture this was taken from and understand the cultural context of how these lines are supposed to be applied. Maybe I get a parable or some type of proverb or example that's going to expand on the information that's being given to me and help apply it better. And I didn't see that in my reading.

"What I've learned from my Black psychology mentors and from Indigenous philosophies is that energy, performance, and behavior in Western colonial systems work from deficit models whereas Indigenous models are strengths-based and proactive. By allowing someone to align with their energy instead of forcing everyone into Western boxes of behavior and calling those who don't fit it deficit or undefined we can have much more fulfilling spiritual and health insights.

"Let's look at the hierarchy issue. By hierarchy, I mean for example, Ra is known to have said things like Generators are the great workers of the world and the Manifestors are sitting on this throne, and the Projectors are the special teachers people get wisdom from.

"So, if the Generators are the workers of the world and he's maybe referring to them as slaves who are working the pyramids or something like that–that's the analogy he used—that's feeding into this eugenics idea that the majority of the people who are the people of color, who are the lower class, who are the Jewish people (or whatever you're looking at, at that time)—they're the ones who were supposed to work for us.

"It gives the impression that Generators are supposed to be working for these Manifestors and Projectors and Reflectors, and the Manifestors, Projectors, and Reflectors are special and superior, and they don't have to work like we do. So that's where eugenics was coming in.

"Then with words like undefined and how that's being applied and the open G Center being lacking: When we use terminology that is representing somebody lacking something in that way or saying that somebody doesn't have the undefined thing, there's a lack of clarity there, and that's where we can get into eugenics.

"Even the terminology—it's literally called Human Design. That should have been the first red flag for y'all. Eugenics was about white people being the superior humans and the others sub-humans. And then the Black people were at the very bottom, and you have these middle humans like the Asians or whoever it is.

"So, the way in which Ra posed Human Design as a catch-all, he went back and forth. In some of his videos, he'd say that people were not being prosperous or, not being good on the path because of not following the Design for them. It's kind of like a shameful tone. But then in other videos he's like, oh–it's not Design, it's just an experiment, do whatever you want.

"What are you saying, are we doing the wrong thing or are we doing whatever we want? If it is really a helpful empowering system, then it should work. There's a difference between something not resonating because it's not calling to you versus something not resonating because it does not work and it's harmful.

"I'm not a numerologist. So it's not resonating in the sense that it's not something that has called me, but I got a numerology reading that was very helpful and accurate for me. Numerology is not my thing; astrology is my thing.

"I think people try and put Human Design in this category of–it just doesn't resonate for me personally, and it's not my thing, versus it's not my thing because it does not accurately look like who I am, and it comes from these roots that just are not applicable to my life and actually are harmful.

"[Some] people have found so much clarity in Human Design, and of course, you're going to find clarity at some points, because like I said, it's rooted in celestial, age-old traditions that are accurate, like astrology, I Ching, and Kabbalah which are accurate. The problem is that people get so lost in that, that they're not aware, especially if they don't have the political understanding or the psychological background of oppression and issues like that. They're going to want to look the other way when people are using the terminology to harm. To be honest, people don't even need a background in political education or organizing/activism to recognize Human Design issues. With Human Design, if you have race, class, or disability struggles, that can be enough to notice the problems.

"When people started critiquing Human Design, sharing videos of the founder, somebody quoted, tweeted it and retweeted it, and said something like, if you don't get it then it's not meant for you, and you're not smart enough to get it. Again, that has a eugenics undertone because it's saying your intelligence is inferior and only certain people will be allowed to understand this.

"Whereas with numerology, even though it's not my thing in that it's not something I've gravitated toward teaching people about, there was nothing I misunderstood about my numerology reading; it was very clear, it was very accurate, and I got everything.

"When people start bringing intelligence into why a person may not like Human Design, that's also another form of eugenics coming in, because you're saying that the person has an inferior intelligence to you. And I don't think people within Human Design are aware of the political and cultural and eugenic implications in the Human Design language and framework that is going around. And we don't see that in other systems.

> "I think another reason why Human Design fans ignore people's concerns of Human Design, besides the fact that they feel it has benefited them, is that in the Western capitalistic colonial society we have grown up in conditions where we do not question the roots of things of honor ancestral roots/lineages of traditions." (Elmina Bell, pers. comm.)

Astrology vs. Human Design

How we are trained in the Human Design system makes all the difference. If we don't have teachers reminding us that we have the entire chart, whether we have definition or openness, we forget to remind ourselves that we are whole beings, having all the parts. We don't speak much in Human Design about having all the parts, and this perspective Elmina brings on how astrology visually shows us the whole and all the parts, is a reminder that as practitioners we want to leave people knowing their wholeness and not what they lack.

> "I'm not really seeing people use astrology in that way, even though there are certain harmful things in astrology that I have critiqued.
>
> "So, for instance, you know about debilities[42] like detriment and fall[43] of a planet. That's something

---

[42] Debilities in Astrology: https://www.astrotheme.com/astrology_planetary-rulerships.php
[43] Detriment in Astrology: A planet positioned in the zodiac sign opposite the sign it rules. https://astrostyle.com/astrology/essential-dignities/

I've critiqued heavily for the same reasons I have to critique Human Design because I feel like classifying energy in that way, especially when you're not looking at the cultural context of how those energies can be used, is kind of harmful.

"If somebody has Mercury in detriment and in Pisces, there's a feeling like their learning might be deficient or they may struggle with learning. Whereas I think no, they just use Pisces energy to learn, which is where I think astrology has an upper hand compared to Human Design because it's not claiming that learning is undefined, or you're lacking this, or you don't have a Sacral for example.

"That was another thing, Human Design describing people as non-Sacral and saying you don't have the thing. Whereas everybody has everything in astrology, so even though nobody will have all twelve signs in their planets, you have the planetary expression of that somewhere in your chart.

"Like you, everybody has an intelligence, which is Mercury. Everybody has an emotional body, which is Moon there's no, 'You don't have this or a non-Sacral, or people lacking a thing,' but people can sometimes, with a detriment and fall situation, describe the thing as being weaker or as deficient.

"And again, when you're not looking at Indigenous perspectives of how planetary themes are going to be expressed, and you're telling somebody that it's weak or that it's debilitated, it doesn't hold. Mercury and Pisces; the dreams; non-linear stuff; vibrational energies; art; vibrations and tones. Indigenous peoples use art a lot to communicate, and dreams.

"They respected knowledge and information because what is Mercury? Information and knowledge. You get a lot of information and knowledge from your dreams, and from vibrations, from art, and from tones; we have very tonal languages. And that's what Mercury is supposed to be ruling. So rather than saying Mercury is in detriment here, you can just say that Mercury represents knowledge intake and information, and whatever sign it's in is the type of information we're using today and keeps it moving.

"And also, I do something that's pretty rare. I combined tropical and sidereal astrology, which most people don't do, most people just use one. I look at things from that holistic perspective of combining them, which the ancient Egyptians actually did in Ancient Kemet. It was called Ancient Kemet by the Black Africans; the Greeks and Romans changed it to Egypt when they were colonizing. They actually use both sidereal and tropical astrology.

"There's not a lot of information on how they use both, but there are records saying that they use sidereal and tropical.

"When you use sidereal and tropical together, a lot of the classifications of detriment and fall don't make sense.

"For instance, I have my Venus in detriment in Scorpio in tropical. When we switched to sidereal, I have the planet at home in Libra where it's strong. You cannot be in detriment and at home at the same time. Another example, Jupiter has fall in Capricorn and in sidereal, it's at home in Sagittarius. This is the type of stuff where people get so caught up in classifying things as good or bad which is a eugenic mentality, which is an obsession of white supremacy, either-or and only-one-right-way power tactics[44], a colonial mentality that they don't look at how different energy can function differently and how it can be helpful.

"I critique every second. I critique psychology. I critique astrology. I would critique everything because I was raised by parents and mentors and professors who were questioning everything. So that's what I'm doing because I'm aware that colonization, white supremacy, and capitalism infiltrate every system. People talk down to me and call me uneducated despite my interdisciplinary background. This often happens to Black MaGes [Black people of marginalized genders] creating new pathways. But I do not answer to naysayers, I answer to my ancestors, my Spirit, and the communities I serve. If I do not critique and offer holistic Indigenous perspectives, this infiltration will

---

[44] https://www.whitesupremacyculture.info/uploads/4/3/5/7/43579015/okun_-_white_sup_culture_2020.pdf

continue. My ancestors' philosophies saw critiques as acts of care and opportunities to learn and grow.

"It's everywhere. It's in the arts. It's in psychology. It's in everything. And that concern again, like I said, with Human Design is that because of the way it was thrown together and the terminology that was used, I think that it poses a stronger threat or is a bit more dangerous.

"In astrology we don't have that 70 percent of the world are Libras and then the other 30 percent are these people who don't have to do this or that. We don't—astrology doesn't—have the non-Sacral thing. Everybody has everything. Everybody has Mercury. Everybody has Venus. You're complete. You're whole. The way of describing that sometimes is off, but there is an understanding in astrology at least, that everybody has everything in them in some way somehow, which is why some people prefer astrology.

"And I've seen some astrologers talk about how, even though Human Design has astrology in it, somehow, and I don't know exactly like all the terms, but some people's astrology clashes with their Human Design.

"Like for me, for instance, I thought it was weird that I had an undefined Throat, which is like communication, and in my chart, my ascendant, my rising, which is a huge identity expression point, I have Mercury, which is about communication conjunct. So to me, I'm defined by my communication a lot, and my communication has to be strong.

"I do have Chiron there, which is like wounded healer energy, also conjunct in my Mercury, but I don't even think they use Chiron in Human Design. And Chiron is also a teacher. So, it's actually a place where you have some level of mastery as well.

"So, I thought that was weird, and other people have pointed out where astrology is saying one thing, and then you get to Human Design and it's saying something else." (Elmina Bell, pers. comm.)

We really appreciate this critical lens and also state that based on this conversation. We feel strongly that the Human Design reading Elmina had, was given by someone who was uninformed of the impact Human Design can have when coming from the lens of lack. Those of us who have worked extensively with this system and who have done thousands of readings would always approach a client with optimism and provide opportunities for potential healing focus. Also, we would clarify that yes, we both look at astrology (tropical and sidereal) and look at Chiron in both astrology and Human Design.

Our Ancestral Positioning: The Black and Brown Experience

Although the BIPOC Human Design leaders are growing in presence, there is still a lack of representation where BIPOC can feel safe enough to approach the system in its entirety. One leader addressing this break from the ancestral perspective is Clarinda Mann, in her Breaking the Chains program. Clarinda utilizes history, astrology, Human Design, and the Quantum Alignment System™ to walk people through the uncomfortable process of looking at their ancestral influences. We talked to Clarinda to better understand her perspective on how Human Design can evolve so that it can better serve all communities, without gaslighting the Black experience.

What Is Missing in Human Design Communities that Can Help BIPOC

"The biggest thing missing in the Human Design community is people of color. I did not see any faces… and I wondered, where are we? I was learning this information and thought this could really be helpful to our communities. So why don't we know about it? I was really dealing with a lot of bitterness and frustration because, first of all, the history. Just the history of how the United States has been with information and with the people of color, especially with Black people.

"I went through a stage of voicing my feelings and frustrations because I would hear people talk about deconditioning, and I would think of my experiences in the world where I walk out the door and I could not 'decondition' having the experience of a Black woman. Before I can be anything else, in every day and everywhere, that's what I am. That's what they see. And it's not Clarinda. It's this Black woman. This person of color; it's always something else to detract from the wholeness of who we are. I think that was the biggest thing.

"When I first joined the Human Design community, I thought where are we? That was what was missing: our voices weren't there. At least I wasn't seeing them when I first came in. That was a hard one for me and I struggled with it because I would hear people talking about their problems and not to detract from their issues with deconditioning, but I could just sit with my mother and talk about the conditioning there and I would think, A lot of people don't have to deal with this, this extra layer of racism." (Clarinda Mann, pers. comm.)

Why Spiritual Knowledge Is Kept from BIPOC

"The reason spiritual knowledge is kept from BIPOC is because it is not white people's problem.

"Why does racism continue? Because people don't feel like it's a part of their issue. They often just brush it off or they don't pay attention. It's not an issue for them. I don't necessarily think that it was just maliciously done, although there could be that too, but it's just not a point of focus to them until it's brought to them. It's not in their sphere of thinking because they have their own bubble that they're in until these problems get made known." (Clarinda Mann, pers. comm.)

When we look at the parts of the Human Design system and BIPOC's experiences with it, there is a lack of acknowledgment of the roots of the divide, and so racism, the enslavement of humans, and the effects of generations post such atrocities must be addressed. BIPOC today experiences these effects, but they are masked in more subtle and less obvious ways to whiteness[45]. Modern society has seen the problems of BIPOC as insular, without understanding or acknowledging that BIPOC community problems are a result of the systems that have contributed to the wealth of those closest to power. For instance, wealth gaps in Black and other communities have a history of oppressive nationwide practices that have prohibited our ancestors from thriving. These practices can be tracked in the United States. Other countries also experience the same colonizing effect, making this a global issue, albeit with a different tone.

How the Transatlantic Slave Trade Affects Us All

> "I speak of my family and my personal experience because that's the one I know for sure. But I also feel quite confident that there are a large number of other people of color that have experiences that are almost exactly the same story and history, because we are in America.

> "I primarily focused on America because they are a world leader and other countries have followed suit quite a bit. Not saying that they are the ones that started the slave trade or slavery, but it definitely became central, and the United States was built on that system.

---

[45] Whiteness: the structures that produce white privilege, the examination of what whiteness is when analyzed as a race, a culture, and a source of systemic racism, and the exploration of other social phenomena generated by the societal compositions, perceptions, and group behaviors of white people. https://en.wikipedia.org/wiki/Whiteness_studies

"Slavery wouldn't have survived without the system of harm to Indigenous people first and then bringing Africans to support the system. This is the foundation of it all. This is the root. So this is a collective issue. The thing is, it doesn't just impact people of color, unbeknownst to non-people of color." (Clarinda Mann, pers. comm.)

The Chart of Slavery in the US and for the World

"I started Breaking the Chains[46] by first running the astrology chart for Newport News, Virginia. I went there and I spent some time there just feeling that place. They have done a lot of research, so I got the estimated date of when the first Africans arrived and looked at what the Human Design energy blueprint looked like. It was the Incarnation Cross of The Sleeping Phoenix.

"I remind people that when we're looking at a snapshot and like astrologically it is for everybody; this energy is not just for Black people. This is the core wound. People often forget that we all as humans are suffering from this core wound. It's going back to lack of self-love, lack of self-worth, and lack of being able to value ourselves and looking at where these patterns really originated.

"But Europeans were also torturing and doing horrible things to each other centuries before they came to America. They've had their own trauma

---

[46] Breaking The Chains is the program that Clarinda developed in utilizing Quantum Alignment System™ to dismantle racism.

that they were carrying for generations that traveled with them. When we start really digging and looking back, we have tons of trauma suffered by all these people; they are hurt, and they hurt people. I'm hurt, and hurt people hurt." (Clarinda Mann, pers. comm.)

White Guilt and Racism in the US

"When people do know about the effects of enslavement, then they say "we must do something." *My Grandmother's Hands*[47] by Resmaa Menakem goes into great detail. He explains it very well in that book; he talks about clean pain and dirty pain.

"Clean pain is when we recognize that there's something wrong and it makes us uncomfortable, but we're going to work through it. Dirty pain is something that I don't want to touch because it's too painful. It hurts so I'm going to avoid it. I think that a lot of times it comes back to some inner guilt by white folks. Where they have to see themselves as helpful and that they are a good person without really getting to the root of the issue or how they're truly feeling inside.

"An example for me that I see is living between the North and the South in the United States.

---

[47] https://centralrecoverypress.com/product/my-grandmothers-hands-racialized-trauma-and-the-pathway-to-mending-our-hearts-and-bodies-paperback

Your Soul Map

> "I like to live in the South. I prefer the South because down here I know where people stand. There's not really a guess if they are racist. I can respect that. I get it. I know. I know where not to go and who's not going to be very friendly toward me. But in the North, it's this subtle kind of racism that has been allowed to pervade through micro-aggressions. There is a sense of 'I'm a good person, I support this cause, I'm helping Black people here.' Instead of facing the real issues, which I feel never get really addressed.

> "This avoidance of the real root of the problem and the root of the issues unconsciously makes someone overcompensate; they come in and try to overdo it because of their own guilt."

Independent of the mixed company in the Human Design communities, there is power that we have as BIPOC. Looking at our own agency of connection to Spirit/Universe/God, whatever it is that you want to call it, is an essential part of taking back our power. Because Clarinda is an astrologer, she explains how planetary influences guide the constrictions of the past and the openings of our current times, specifically around religion.

Religion as Safety and Security

> "Religion is one of those foundational principles. When we're looking at the hierarchy of needs, when your safety and security are disrupted, it's very hard and things collapse, and so religion has been such a place of safety and security. For so long it has been the protection of the community and that's where people got together.

"You are a united front in a community, you had the same view and belief that you shared, and you knew you were going to be supported there. So, to start stripping that away is hard in a world that doesn't always treat you so well outside of that. Our Christian people will treat you better. People find it so hard to break free from that. And then you've got the internal battle that goes on. So, you ask yourself What's true? What's not and how do I know? How do I trust this?

"You don't know unless you can develop the trust in your own Spirit, your own higher self which you don't really get to develop in religion. In religion, you're giving all your authority out to an outside source. You're not really taught about inner authority. You're taught that 'I'm a dirty rag, I'm meek and lowly' so you stay humble. All of those things contradict what we're trying to instill in someone when we're teaching them Human Design and their Strategy and empowerment." (Clarinda Mann, pers. comm.)

Evolving Spirituality in the Black Community

"I have my Sun in Gate 37[48]. Community is huge for me. I'm going through a lot of these things right now, so there are active examples of this whole thing. I have some aunts and my family grew up very Christian, very church based.

---

[48] Gate 37: Harmony within community.

"They see Human Design as witchcraft. 'Clarinda is doing the devil's work,' they say. My grandparents were supportive, but they passed on, but my aunts see me as a threat to my mother because I encouraged my mother to do what she wants to do and not what she doesn't want to. They feel like I take her away from them. It's this hook that they have on it. I realized my own struggle with being with other Black women and where the root of that came from within my own family. And I also know that it was designed that way too. There was a designer. Turning each other against each other, but even in my own family, seeing it play out and how I felt like, *Y'all aren't my people.*

"We're kin and we're blood, but I don't feel like my family, and, like, I don't feel seen here. I don't feel like I can be me here. I've found that I would like to build a community. That was what broke my heart so much because I wanted to be able to be myself in these places with others.

"I really just happened to realize that I'm still doing my shadow work too, for sure… but I'm just feeling broken-hearted sometimes. The level of disconnection that has been instilled in the community, to tear it apart and almost feeling like, What am I supposed to do now?

"How do I go about building a community of like-minded individuals that can really be compasssionate? Because what I found is that my family is extremely judgmental. They will ostracize you if they don't agree with what you're doing and it's very hard to build a community for me, I have the 44/26 too.

"I just can't. I like authenticity. I like to be truthful. I want to be able to be myself. And so it's hard to build community when you can't do that. And then there's this other divide of it that is: I want to build a strong community.

"How do we heal this? I don't know. I'm kind of asking the question again because I don't really know the answer exactly yet on how to create these kinds of communities. Now, I just feel like I need to be a strong voice and use the parts of my chart the way they're designed, to bring my message; to bring the message out and share and know that and trust that the people, the right people are going to come and that's really hard, to allow and trust and believe and let be.

"I am working on that. That's what I have to do; otherwise, I'm going to be burned out and I can't do anything for anybody else. I have to really think about how to use my energy wisely, especially being a Projector. It's how we're designed. We are here to learn how to use energy wisely and building community takes a lot, but it also takes people that want to be a part of a community—what community do they want to be a part of? And that it can't be by force." (Clarinda Mann, pers. comm.)

Connecting to Spirit and Pluto Influence

"We have to listen to our Spirit—that's always to me first and foremost, and I think that for Black people

> especially, we have lost the connection to the Spirit in some ways like a disconnection. When you look at the word religion it comes from Latin, which means to bind back together.

> "That indicates that there's something that's been unbound. This connection that's been lost. The book *When Things Fall Apart*[49] by Pema Chödrön, talks about when Christianity came into Africa. It was this stripping away of old identities and replacing them with Christian beliefs, becoming the only trusted foundation." (Clarinda Mann, pers. comm.)

The previous generations of Black mothers and grandmothers who have gone through assimilating the experience of generational enslavement have tried to find peace through religion. Clarinda looks at the effects of Pluto (as above, so below) to understand the attachment that her mother and grandmothers have to a religion.

> "I can't let that go. I see the stronghold in my mother's generation. My mother was born in 1954. That generation of people born around that Pluto and Libra generation as being the bridge between the old and new where you start seeing people stepping outside of the organized religion, more open-minded too, more open to other things and other possibilities, outside of religion. Pluto and Virgo are a stronghold. When we look at Virgo and

---

[49] https://pemachodronfoundation.org/product/when-things-fall-apart-book/

its connection to religion, I see that really strongly with my mother's generation.

"It's very scary for them. And even when I left the church, it hurts to have everything you believed in torn down, taken away like... you know, that's painful. Everything that you thought was true is not. And so, I do have to remind myself of that and be compassionate toward them as well because I understand, you know, if it wasn't for religion, we might not have got through slavery, you know, if it wasn't for them Negro hymns and spirituals; that was part of their resiliency that kept them going and able to get up and it's hard to let go of it. I look at Pluto as kind of being the planet that is showing the more, it's an outer planet collective.

"When Pluto is moving and shifting, I see major theme shifts in a generational kind of thing. So, Pluto will be moving into Aquarius in 2023/2024 in and out those couple of years, that generation is going to be quite different from the Capricorn." (Clarinda Mann, pers. comm.)

The Pluto transit is a revolutionary time of removing unnecessary aspects and forces us to deepen our view in areas of life. It is associated with rebirth energy.

"When we have those periods shifts, we start seeing people born with a little bit of a different viewpoint and a dynamic that they bring in as a group.

"Although we could talk about other BIPOC experiences and we could gather historical examples of other groups who have been oppressed, we do not want to dilute the importance of the Black experience." (Clarinda Mann, pers. comm.)

> "If Black women were free, it would mean that everyone else would have to be free since our freedom would necessitate the destruction of all the systems of oppression."[50]
>
> —Barbara Smith and the Black feminist visionaries of the Combahee River Collective

Making it Work for Us

Making Human Design work for us is a balance of both approaching the system with respect to its theory and origin and also recognizing the added layer in our collective and individual implementation. The system has validity; it's working, and it works for the people with the most power, but as BIPOC we have to not shun the system because of its creator and be more open to the validity of its usefulness. We have to acknowledge that it was started by a white man when capitalism was rampant, yet it is a valid blueprint for how we can maximize our lives. We have to make a decision to use and adapt the system in a way that fits us. We have to stop cutting our noses to spite our faces when many of these systems can be a gateway to our liberation. We have to stop resisting.

---

[50] https://www.newyorker.com/news/our-columnists/until-black-women-are-free-none-of-us-will-be-free

How to Promote Human Design to the Black Community

"I have to decide where to plug in, where to put my energy, and where to not put it. I have to learn, as a Projector, when I'm really truly recognized and seen for what I offer and when I'm not, and to not go into those places until I'm invited.

"I am working with this word recognition because it's not like I need to be seen or like 'I'm the best.' So waiting for people to see me and stepping back, maybe presenting something out there and stepping back and letting them sit with it. I used to try to force it. I would be wanting to preach to everybody about breaking free of all that. You know, like question church, because it's so strongly instilled in the Black community. I would get upset– why can't you see what this has done and how the system has been used?

"That's my first thing. The second thing is by leading by example, and I have a 6 Line in my Profile and it's being the Role Model. Let me show you that it's working because people believe what they see; it's easier for them to follow that example.

"Have the courage to step out of those systems, stand firmly in what you believe in, and then show them what you're doing. The proof is in the pudding kind of thing and lets that be the thing that speaks for me, instead of me being out here trying to forcefully push my will onto people.

"Because when I do that, then I'm just perpetuating a system that I'm trying to break free from." (Clarinda Mann, pers. comm.)

Generational Opening

"This healing is generational. When I talk about my aunts, the oldest being seventy, there's that level of that layer there as well.

"But my younger cousins, like they often come and they're calling me to come over. They want to talk and have these discussions, they're more open to it. I see that, as well as my mom. I don't think that my other aunts will be open to it. I don't think because it feels so uncertain and unsafe.

"Religion is safe to them. They feel safe. They're in their comfort zone. So, the biggest thing I can do is work on my issues and heal my bitterness and just be able to come at them with compassion for where they're at and keep it there. For the ones that really want to move forward, I'm here for that too. That's the biggest thing I can do. I think the biggest thing is an individual journey to a certain extent because we've got to do that healing for ourselves. I like to get really honest with myself about what I'm feeling. If I'm feeling bitter and angry and I need to figure out why and get to the bottom of why. Because me sitting here and not being truthful about it with myself is not helping anyone. Bitterness for Projectors is not nice energy. It's strong. I don't want to be repelling people away from me so I've got to work on my stuff and learn to create these spaces where I can be unconditionally accepting of people, who they are, where they are, and just let it, you know, kind of work itself out. I do believe in a higher power. I do not think of it in the same way as I did like in religion, but I do believe that there is a higher force that's at work.

"I have to trust in the right timing." (Clarinda Mann, pers. comm.)

Healing Within Our BIPOC Communities

"There's a lot of division in our communities as well.

"For example, my family has mixed backgrounds, but it doesn't matter, in the United States it doesn't matter. You're Black. In the household, I'm the darkest one in my family, but when we go out in the world with each other and interact, some of my harshest experiences have not been with white people, but they've been with BIPOC.

"I've had Latin people that just started speaking Spanish to me, like in Florida. And when I lived in Texas or if they saw me with my husband, they would give me these funny looks. There is division there too, you know, within those communities. We need to work on strengthening that kind of community; the people of color need to strengthen their communities within each other. I think that if we can do that kind of work, it's gonna help facilitate being able to share this information in these groups. It's not just with the white people and the people of color, but it's also within the groups of color because there are categories of color with Black being at the very bottom. It is the lowest on the spectrum and then maybe Latin next and then Indigenous, and I would say that Asian would be the next under white. Not all people of color are the same. And within the groups of people of color, we have huge divisions that keep us from being a unified front.

"I'm seeing a shifting, you know, I'm seeing this happen, this pattern. I think that it will continue to shift, but we need to focus on these communities as well and build them up. And I think Human Design can help us do that for sure. But with all of those cultures, especially Latin and Black, religion is a strong thing." (Clarinda Mann, pers. comm.)

The Human Design Camps

While writing this book the topic came up around the purist and the new age Human Design practitioners. There has been heavy discourse on what is right and what is wrong, and we felt it was important for us to dig deeper into this conversation as we consider what would most support the evolution of Human Design so that it can work for all kinds of people. Listen to Jasmine Nnenna, Capricorn Sun, Pisces Moon, Leo Rising, 3/5 Generator, speak about the labeling and segmentation of "fundamentalist" versus "pop" Human Design in the community.

"I was actually deeply in love with Human Design. All ten toes in and I didn't have any qualms. I would read the book and think Yeah, this is a little outrageous, but a lot of spiritual teachers before us have been very eccentric. So I never really questioned it. At that time I was doing a lot of kundalini yoga and Yogi Bhajan was very eccentric, a borderline all-the-things (not good) teacher, so also was Osho.

"I just thought it was like the times; All of the teachers that were coming out in these times had this air about them. It actually wasn't until recently, in the last year, on social media, when there started to become these camps set up; source material and Pop Human Design, and some people called them 'fundamentalists,' the 'true' Ra successors.

"It seemed like they were taking the stance as the chosen ones. To this day, I genuinely don't understand what that energy is about. If you truly feel that you're being called to be inside of a lineage of teaching and feel called to be fruitful while continuing on a legacy, you would be in the energy of compassion and inclusion, wanting all people to be aware, integrated, informed, and embodied; focused on what you are trying to leave behind, and honoring the teachings that you got from the teacher [Ra].

"Not until recently did I begin to feel it is all questionable. I also can't imagine that your Strategy and Authority told you to divide people. I have a hard time believing that anyone's Strategy and Authority would tell them to cause emotional harm.

"There are different camps with communities of Human Design that perpetuate: You're teaching it wrong or you're sharing information wrongly and it's hurting people... It's like a right and wrong camp. For me, all information is integrated through the person so differently.

"I mean we all went to school. We all learned the Pythagorean theorem. They tried to teach us the exact same thing. And none of us ever used it. So why not teach and learn something that we can integrate into our own unique lives? Maybe some people want to go as far as determination[51] and maybe some people are satisfied with Type, Strategy, and Authority.

"The Human Design teachings are inherently, mentally defined, and so it can lend itself to be translated in a way that would suit people so they can digest it more easily. We always talk about spiritual medicines having to be sweet so that it's easier for the person to take in. I feel that's the intention with what people would call 'pop' Human Design or 'spiritual' Human Design. There's a lot of talk with the 'purists or fundamentals' that Human Design is not spiritual, which I understand [that Ra said it's mechanics and it's scientific].

"While I understand that we are Spirit, it's very hard to break apart and say, for instance, your iPhone is inherently technology, but the genius that came down through the body to make this iPhone was Spirit. So, you can't say that the iPhone just made itself straight from the technology. It's that kind of awareness that I would love to see brought more

---

[51] Determination is a second wave of Human Design concepts on lifestyle choices around digestion.

into the Human Design space, but I also understand that no growth happens without conflict. That's also what's happening; more people are starting to wonder if they would be that rigid. Because in the original, the source materials, there were no Types and then Ra made Types to make the information more available.

"The system is moving further than it has been. I almost feel like we have to keep doing that because not only is our time attention span moving down from reading blogs to reading seven-second blurbs, but we generally are also changing as a collective.

"I have been labeled as 'pop' HD and have known people who have been blocked by source material people. I cannot imagine that if Ra were alive, he would condone people blocking each other because of their personal translation of the system. There are so many things that I read and so many seminars and workshops that he gave where he actually admitted, 'I don't have the time and energy to penetrate certain concepts so I'm going to leave them. I'm literally going to just talk briefly about them, leave them, and then whoever follows their Strategy and Authority to find this perspective, or this idea can penetrate it further. They will eventually bring more information and depth to this specific topic.' Human Design is not a one-person thing; it's a collective thing." (Jasmine Nnenna, pers. comm.)

Whiteness Consciousness

> *"The problem is that white people see racism as conscious hate, when racism is bigger than that. Racism is a complex system of social and political levers and pulleys set up generations ago to continue working on the behalf of whites at other people's expense, whether whites know/like it or not. Racism is an insidious cultural disease. It is so insidious that it doesn't care if you are a white person who likes Black people; it's still going to find a way to infect how you deal with people who don't look like you.*
>
> *"Yes, racism looks like hate, but hate is just one manifestation. Privilege is another. Access is another. Ignorance is another. Apathy is another. And so on. So, while I agree with people who say no one is born racist, it remains a powerful system that we're immediately born into. It's like being born into air: you take it in as soon as you breathe. It's not a cold that you can get over.*
>
> *"There is no anti-racist certification class. It's a set of socioeconomic traps and cultural values that are fired up every time we interact with the world. It is a thing you have to keep scooping out of the boat of your life to keep from drowning in it. I know it's hard*

work, but it's the price you pay for owning everything." [52]

–Scott Woods

"That's whiteness consciousness. It's in the breath. It's in every breath and it's in all Black people. It's in all people of color. We are decolonizing from that even to see ourselves clearly.

"It is the ultimate deconditioning. I think Human Design is liberating itself. I always imagine these things are their own entities. I feel like the more people that give their life force energy to growing, expanding, and connecting to Human Design, it will continue to blossom." (Jasmine Nnenna, pers. comm.)

Liberation

"We don't have a racism problem. We are all the same race. It's like humans are fighting each other. When people say, I want to be anti-racist. You can never be anti-racist. your race is human. How can you be anti-human? What you should be saying is you want to be in celebration of Black liberation.

"When we talk about Black liberation, then we can do something, and we know where we're going. Every decision then is in continuity with the values of Black liberation, not with anti-racism. This is why nothing is happening with anti-racism.

---

[52] https://www.goodreads.com/quotes/8784483-the-problem-is-that-white-people-see-racism-as-conscious

"Anti-racism is a wall. I wish we would see that we are not getting anywhere because we're not using the correct words. Words are the breadth of God that allows us to see deeper than anything we could ever know.

"As soon as you say Black liberation, people have ideas. We can start. We can start ideating and brainstorming on what to build in honor of Black liberation. When you say anti-racist, you are a lost cause, it's a lost cause like you have nothing.

"If you want to read another white fragility book then nothing happens; however, I really just want people to read the meanings of words; words are the codes to set you free, to set us free." (Jasmine Nnenna, pers. comm.)

Part 4: Adaptation and Embodiment in Human Design

Capitalism and the Promise of a New Economy

Astrology Through the Ages

In Human Design there is speculation that there is a Solar Plexus mutation in 2027 which would also coincide with a change in how commerce and systems operate. Let's look to the backbone of the Human Design system, astrology, to better understand what the approximate 2,000-year astrological ages say about impending changes.

Ancient civilizations show us that scientists and observers of nature have been following the pattern in the stars. So much so that cultures such as ancient Egyptians pivoted worship to deities that resembled the stars. From the

Taurus era (sacred cows and Goddess Hathor[53]) to the Aries era (Sun worship, such as God Ra[54]) to Piscean (the Christ) and now in the dawn of the Aquarius era[55]. Other ancient mythologies, such as the Mayan calendar and Hindu yugas confirm a shift in the world.

Capitalism

Human Design offers an opportunity for us to work with our natural Design and thrive as we honor ourselves in all environments, and capitalism is at odds with this liberation lens. Nine-to-five schedules and the company culture are killing individual Aura Types that have different values and ideals for living and working. We have become beings who work to live rather than beings who live to work.

Most of us don't know what it costs for us to live within the structure of capitalism. We have a lot of perceptions of what it is and what it is not but rarely do we take a closer look at how it imprisons or liberates us. Capitalism is not going anywhere in the near future; if it goes away, the United States and capitalist nations do not exist. We have to figure out how to live in this materialistic society within the life we currently live.

Within the anti-racist conversation there is an ethos that if we are in support of Black liberation, we are against capitalism. In an ideal world, we can all see how this is true,

---

[53] Hathor: cow horned Egyptian goddess.
[54] Ra: Egyptian sun god.
[55] There are different calculations: some say it began in 2012.

yet most of us are not at a place where we have the privilege to opt out. Opting out is a privilege.

Capitalism has some people believe that if they opt out, they will be taken care of, but that can be a constrictive existence. That option to be homesteaders is ideal for some, but not for many of us who want to stay connected to modern civilization. We all have different choices and different access points to such lifestyles, and many of us want to create solutions that work for the common person.

As Trudi Lebrón, author of *The Antiracist Business Book*, points out that someone has to fund the movement. Sometimes the movement is our own personal liberation.

Something that non-BIPOC don't always understand is that for Black and Brown people, wealth is safety; it is protection from the system, and it is the doorway to overcome all oppressive practices. When we have access to wealth, we have the ability to solve problems. Wealth may seem like a universal solution for all, but for BIPOC it levels the playing field of life. When a non-BIPOC makes $150,000, it is not the same as a Black person making the same money. The laws and the practices of the land do not make equal revenue as an equalizer.

Wealth is resistance because typically BIPOC extends the wealth to others; it is our community-centric approach that is a constant reminder that when we create wealth, we do it for ourselves, for representation, and to tangibly contribute to the liberation of others that look like us.

Wealth, Guilt, and Creating Accessibility

For those of us who are interested in creating new world economies, wealth is a complex subject; we either want to accumulate wealth to be the stewards of the distribution of such wealth, or we reject the system for multiple reasons, including how we want our work to be accessible to others. This is a convoluted topic and the only thing we want to say about this is that it is an individual answer. What we know for sure is that many of us need to be prosperous to overflow. In our community, we are more interested in holding people's financial desires and helping them create models where they can develop accessibility from a solid financial foundation. This exploration and tension we each have could be related to the Solar Plexus mutation where the initiation of the system begins with Gate 50, the maternal Gate of Values for the Community[56].

BIPOC Hiding Our Well-being and Guilt with Wealth

In order for BIPOC to overcome systemic oppression and align to the path of abundance, well-being, and the right community, we have to address the truth of the past that affects us today. The trauma experienced by Black people in building wealth and having it burned down and destroyed runs through the veins of today, i.e., Seneca Village (also known as Central Park), Black Wall Street[57], etc. It takes great effort to stay focused on building wealth while

---

[56] Interview with Karen Curry Parker.
[57] https://travelnoire.com/black-american-towns-hidden and https://www.youtube.com/watch?v=pTSRqTZ0EQQ

contending with unconscious epigenetic programs and the reality of a world that is threatened by Black wealth. Also, immigrants and other Brown people experience conscious or unconscious societal expectations that diminish the potential of the individual.

When BIPOC does overcome the constraints of systemic oppression we find ourselves still being cautious and can be a bit guarded because of how we are perceived in the world. Unless we create a supportive community, life can feel isolating. And as we evolve and become wealthier, we can have a tendency to feel guilty about our well-being.

We each have to acknowledge and contend with the challenges before us, and still deserve to stay focused and devote ourselves to our dreams and our goals and be with people that are vested in fully celebrating our success.

Before We Create a New Economy

What Human Design shows us is that we can personally liberate ourselves and that personal liberation can be expressed in the world and in the economy. This is why knowing your own chart and how you are designed can help you liberate yourself in a capitalistic society. Even as Generators and Manifesting Generators you have protocols to follow. The Human Design system tells Projectors to sit back and wait for invitations, but capitalism demands the hustle. Knowing your chart allows you to know what will work for you and know how you can excel in any given situation.

It is clear that most of us know the status quo needs to change and it is challenging to change a system overnight.

Those of us vested in a change can recognize that we need a transition plan. This plan can include bridging this gap with more equitable solutions and also encouraging BIPOC to focus on personal wealth, should they want that.

Rewriting the Rules for Energetic Success

In Human Design each Aura Type has a *signature* theme that when pursuing that signature, they are able to operate in the highest capacity with minimal inner resistance. The signatures are an energetic push felt by the person and it is individualistic in nature. This means that one person's expression of the *signature* can look and feel very different from another person's.

Manifestors: Your signature theme is peace or some type of sense of contentment or ease. You want to experience life without interference or resistance, in total flow and connection.

Projectors: Your signature theme is success and recognition. You want to feel appreciated and to have experiences that acknowledge the highest form of who you are.

Generators/Manifesting Generators: Your signature theme is satisfaction. It is about having experiences where inner and outer energy is allocated in ways that feel good—feeling alive, dynamic, and connected with the constant exchange with life.

Reflectors: Your signature theme is surprise. Surprise in the sense of discovering something new about yourself and the world around you. You are in constant search of pockets of joy in the mundane.

To succeed as a whole, we need to tap back into how the individual can succeed. Every Aura Type has a signature, and each has its own way of birthing that into reality using the Human Design system to define what satisfaction, peace, success, and surprise look like for the individual.

As a Manifestor, what does peace look and feel like? As a Projector what does success look and feel like? As a Generator Type, what does satisfaction look and feel like? And as a Reflector what does surprise look and feel like?

It is key for us to define what the signatures mean for us individually so that we can access all of the systems to our benefit. Human Design gets to be practical in our day-to-day life, but also, we get to push the envelope of our liberated selves in the work place. Whether we work in traditional corporate settings or have our own businesses.

Let's talk about capitalism and how companies operate. We should be able to work how we want to work. As long as we get our work done, we should be able to be liberated in our lives. With the use of technology and the way we learn, we are more efficient as a whole. Organizations talk about innovation, but in reality, they do not want the spaciousness needed to be creative. Humans are being squeezed for all they have. There is a predatory practice to hire people with minimal experience to pry every ounce of their youth, depriving individuals of real growth.

Human Design allows an individual to align their authentic energy in the workplace and to become the most effective and efficient participants in any work environment. When leadership trusts the genius of the individual to contribute to the whole, not only do we foster innovation but also work satisfaction and a sense of individual and collective purpose. Depending on the circuitry of the individual and how their aura interacts with others, the synergy of the group or department is understood and can be utilized to the highest capacity.

The Human Design system allows us to communicate effectively in work environments that previously squashed the individual voice and were complacent with the way things were. This system allows people to express their true gifts, so they can liberate their creative genius.

Together we have worked with small businesses and corporations to help their teams work with more synergy, honoring the individuals in the groups, fostering environments of true innovation, and resulting in revenue growth and a sense of belonging for employees.

Freedom to Manage in Professional Spaces

Mindfulness, work life balance, health, sensitivity training, and other aspects of accounting for the humanity in each person in the workplace have begun to be more prevalent in work environments. Although still leading edge and beginning to influence individuals, both astrology and Human Design can also help orient individuals, groups, and companies to greater individual, professional, and collective success. We have seen the implementation work well for teams. Here are some examples of how Human Design particularly can benefit companies.

Human Design Consulting by Aycee

I was contacted by an online marketer who runs a multimillion-dollar business with a team of fifteen who worked virtually. The impact of the 2020 pandemic resulted in heightened stress for this team; communication breakdowns, and energetic dynamics changed, and the group was faced with a crossroads on how to move forward with the team.

Using Human Design we analyzed the individuals, their gifts, and challenges within their roles, and I discovered through their charts that many of the team members were not being utilized to use their strengths and were exalting their less consistent energy. After discussing how each person would be set up to thrive, we developed a strategy where key members were able to communicate their wants and needs as well as operate in the most effective ways in their roles.

This resulted in a better communication process, and everyone felt safe to be themselves and receive support from management so they could unfold in their positions more effectively. This ultimately increased the corporation's bottom line.

Conscious Commerce by Asha

We can all agree that the extractive practices of today's workplace and the devaluing practices that support profit margins over the ability of individuals to earn a thriving wage must end. We are at a crossroads of how we shift to a different model that is regenerative to the individual, the company, society, and the Earth. In my attempt to find solutions I am stewarding a model that aims to allow people to feel good, companies to create wealth, and a ceremonial process to design ways of creating equitable practices and giving back ventures.

Human Design plays a key role in this model. Companies are able to serve the individual needs and wants to be based on people's Design and trust the creative process of new synergy to increase revenue and profits. Creating practices that honor the mechanics of Human Design creates environments of safety; people can truly see each other and support each other. The value of this baseline is unknown to most of us, and we are in the experiment of what it means to support the individual for the greater good. In this overflow, we then have the capacity to shift away from fear-based goal setting to creative and global impact-driven models. In this model we are taking things further than the standard personal growth in companies; this is about exploring reparation and regenerative practices.

This is why tools such as Human Design are so important and helpful in business. This understanding fosters prioritizing the energetics of individuals, giving corporations the opportunity to create work environments that allow freedom of self-expression, and it ultimately helps the bottom line. Old models of business disregard the importance of self-fulfillment, but the new forward-thinking economy and workplace demand the space for the true growth of individuals, on their own terms. This model of business creates company cultures people are excited to work in. Part of the passion we have is to infuse Human Design based approaches into the workplace because we see the potential when individual aspirations and company goals align.

Embodiment of the Aura Type: How Astrology and Human Design Play a Practical Role

These two systems, especially since astrology is foundational to Human Design, play a key role in the puzzle of how we create commerce that is sacred for a quadruple win (individual, company, society, and the Earth).

Astrology allows us to see our potential for earning with the tools to utilize our strengths and not succumb to society's expectations. When we look at our charts, we can fully see who we are in relation to the stars and our time of birth and capitalize on our unique expression unapologetically.

Part 5: The Charts from a BIPOC Perspective

Understanding Your Chart

If you do not know where to start, start first knowing about your Aura Type, then your Profile, then learn your *open* and *defined centers*, and then finally the activated *gates*. Knowing yourself intimately goes beyond knowing your personality; the Human Design chart provides insight into the mystery of your existence, how you were intended to shine, how you were intended to heal, how you were intended to grow, and the practical ways to uniquely make decisions. Your astrology and your Human Design show the way you were intended to be without the conditioning and the programs of this existence and showcase the potential of your soul in this lifetime.

A Few Steps to Incorporate the Process of Knowing Yourself

First, practice living in your Strategy and Authority by speaking your truth without overthinking (Manifestors), trusting and responding (Generator Types), allowing for invitations to come (Projectors), and feeling into a Lunar cycle to come to your answer (Reflectors). Your Authority is going to allow you to make decisions that will help your life move forward and that feel good to you and do not go against the grain but rather create the space for you to flow. Your Authority provides you with an understanding of how to make decisions that will consistently serve your highest good.

When you understand and embody your Strategy and Authority, next move into your Profile. This provides how you engage with life; how you are in relationships with others and how you execute your vision. It is important to understand the nuances of your conscious and unconscious Profile because it is the key to your alignment with your chart. You will gain better understanding of how you naturally unfold in the world.

With this book we hope to have given you a map to your soul and a starting point onto a more aligned journey; both honoring your walk as BIPOC and giving yourself permission to be fully expressed and thriving in the world.

This is not a one-time fix-all; this is a journey you have to be willing to take. We may have years of undoing to slowly embody new realities and dreams.

Human Design Aura Types Redefined

Life is about facing and overcoming ourselves over and over again: inner limitations, fears, traumas, and our conditioned self.

On our path we are faced with decisions that determine whether we move forward being at war, in peace, or in resolution with ourselves and the rest of the world.

The first forty years can feel like a folding inward, feeling into who we are so that after four decades on this planet we give ourselves full permission to exist standing fully in our own truth and authenticity, with the ability to create without inhibition, constantly refining the quality of our life.

This doesn't mean that the first forty years have been lost, but rather have been an unfolding of the journey we have taken to define what is truth and what makes us whole.

The theme of our Aura Type is universal and a practical guide for being in relationship with the Universe.

It is a guideline and does not discount upbringing and societal conditioning or trauma.

When You Are a Generator

You are here to become an expert in your craft. The journey can look like one of evolution until there is a plateau. At that plateau there is inquiry, and the next piece of the expertise puzzle becomes the theme. You tend to feel frustrated and blocked in this plateau. Because of the Sacral energy, you can be unaware of appropriate levels of "enough is enough"; just because you can, doesn't mean you should.

Due to your non-motorized Throat Center, which is the center for authentic voice, creative expression, and actualizing your purpose, you do require the co-creative energy of others, who can bring the motorized collective Throat.

The plateau can be perceived as a "dark night of the soul" or a moment to pause and wait for the Universe to offer you the next piece to achieve next-level skills. When you are faced with this plateau, it is your job to lean into it and look for the clues that will lead you to the next step in your path. You cannot move forward unless you open up completely and exhaust all avenues and all possibilities for the next level you are trying to attain; this level is achieved when satisfaction is felt, not necessarily when the mind is satisfied.

When the clues and the signs are received, it is imperative for you to be fully connected to your Sacral response—your yes and your no.

This does not mean that you are locked into an identity or a job or a specific craft; it means that there is a theme that carries you and you have the ability to learn from your previous incarnations and utilize it, however it is you want to redefine yourself. Remember there is a fine line between continuing your journey of expertise and balancing your fantasy to burn it all down; you need to decide when you will be satisfied. And part of this refinement is clarifying what satisfaction is to you and what it feels and looks like. The life that a Generator leads is a *journey*; surrender to the journey and let go of any expectations of overnight success or growth. Becoming an expert is a process.

Take-home: You are on the path of greatness. In this path there are plateaus; stay open and faithful to your next level of growth and what you believe.

When You Are a Manifesting Generator

You really hold the key to progressive change, but you don't know it because you are distracted by all the things that may not serve your highest good. As a Manifesting Generator with this type of power, it is really important for you not to waste time with things that don't light you up and to be open to the ideas and pings that are in alignment with what you are already doing. There is an energy you carry that makes you want to accomplish many feats versus focusing on what will bring you the most reward.

On the flip side, these twists and turns inform and flavor the path and if you can bring an attitude of both exploration and stick-to-it-ness, you won't flounder but rather actualize this power of change. The balance here is to allow yourself to explore, especially during your first forty years of life, and then focus on developing the quality of your yes. Does this yes align with the bigger vision? Have you gathered all the pieces that fully inform and contribute to the transformation you want to offer the world?

Take-home: We invite you to have grace with your path and know that the frustration you feel can also be an indication that you are alive and in the trenches of life, testing your correct fit, passion, and true calling. Frustration doesn't have to be a bad thing, just an indicator that there *is* energy that is wanting release and that a solution awaits you as you stay in the game of life. Frustration is also an opportunity to explore if you are involved in too many things that do not serve you and a prompt to fine-tune your efforts.

With this power, comes great ethics. The power of evolving new systems is beautiful but when unconscious, it can be messy. The exploration of tapping into different samplings of energy is a valid exploration for Manifesting Generators but it is one that when unchecked can create more harm than good.

When You Are a Projector

It is important for you to understand you are not being overlooked, unseen, or unheard, but it is the Universe's way to give you time to become your most authentic self until the right invitation is presented to you. The wisdom you hold has the power to affect the course of someone's life and this power is one that requires that the recipient be fully vested in the message. When the opportunity arises, your ability for efficiency removes all time barriers. The way you see and penetrate into the psyche and soul of another is what makes "waiting for the invitation" important. The experience can be intense so the best way to honor this is to wait until someone is ready to receive this.

The way to arrive at this level of confidence is to overcome the hurts of the past when you were not fully seen and heard. When you heal the way that you received their unreadiness, you can settle into your rightful place of being the *sage* of your community.

Take-home: You *are* the sage. Wait for others to be ready for you and then the wisdom that you have can be fully received. Be intentional and deliberate with your energy.

When You Are a Manifestor

You are the spark in any community. You are the person that initiates us into the directness from the Universe to the material plane. You have the ability to believe. Once you focus on an idea or a way of life, reality does not exist for you; you are able to see it through to your liking. Believe this, heal the conditioning of the world around you, and surround yourself with people who can help you complete and finish all the projects you begin.

You are the direct channel of universal energy, and it is important for you to know that your voice and opinion are to be spoken, not for validation, but to inform people of what is going to happen. Do not get caught up in life with the opinions of others, but rather do everything possible to strengthen your voice.

If your childhood was one where your power was suppressed, you have the opportunity to advocate for yourself and reclaim your power.

Take-home: You are the initiator; own it. You are the catalyst for creative movement and by surrounding yourself with people who can execute your vision, you will facilitate your place in the community and world. If this feels beyond your reach, your number one job is to work on believing in the potency of your truth.

When You Are a Reflector

There is so much here on this earthly plane for you; the uniqueness of your being can make you feel like an outcast and misunderstood. Your love of humanity and your vision of what is possible are important in this world. People may disappoint you and your vision may feel out of touch, but your divine place on this earthly plane is to be the barometer for what is and to hold the vision for what could be.

It is important that you practice self-preservation and surround yourself with people who can hold space for your emotions, your ever-changing energetics, and your vision for the world.

Pay close attention to how you feel in spaces, communities, and life and work environments.

Take-home: You are a humanitarian by nature, so it is important that you make sure you are continuously advocating for yourself first before going out in the world to advocate for others. This applies to all Types but perhaps a bit more for you: Be fully resourced physically, mentally, emotionally, and spiritually before you help others.

Redefining Authorities to Include Emotional Well-being

1. Sacral
2. Emotional
3. Splenic
4. Ego/Heart
5. Self/Identity/G Center
6. Mental/Environmental
7. Lunar

Human Design does not address the way Authorities in the Human Design system bypass systematic trauma and nervous system regulation. As BIPOC with ancestral history, we have no control over the system. And when we follow the guidance on using Authority for decision-making, there is an added layer making it harder for us to use our Authority in an aligned manner. Although we have more access to emotional and spiritual connection, we have been entrained to suppress our emotions, especially in mixed company. The world at large feels unsafe for us to be fully expressed. Many of us have been taught to suppress our emotions as a survival mechanism. And before the veil of suppression of the system is lifted, we struggle to identify or feel the wave of emotion, since emotions are a threat to our survival, and hence it is harder to trust, such as for an Emotional Authority.

A prime example would be how we, as Black women, are not seen as delicate and sensitive creatures; we are positioned as strong and hard, with labels that denote us as not being allowed to access politically correct emotions. The layer of emotions can seem like a universal problem we all face, but depending on our identity, this factor is heightened; there is epigenetic wiring that prohibits access to freely exploring emotions. Although we feel that we as BIPOC have more natural access to the emotional and spiritual realms once that is allowed, we have a societal barrier to overcome. When we allow ourselves to fully feel and be seen in our feelings, we are able to regulate our nervous system and are then able to trust the wave of emotions.

Human Design Authority gives us the opportunity to have a pathway to filter our emotions. For instance, if we have Emotional Authority, we need to experiment with our unique emotional wave, heal from societal programming around our feelings, and then negotiate space to feel the wave and honor it.

Sacral Authority

When you have a defined Sacral Center (not combined with Solar Plexus Center definition), you are intended to make decisions prioritizing your Sacral response, meaning that you are constantly in relationship to life, and your job is to pay attention to how your Sacral is turned on or turned off by each situation.

In Human Design we talk about the Sacral Authority with the sound, *uh-huh* and *uh-uh*, but what we aren't talking about is the tone, the desire, and the power within the womb center. What Traditional Human Design has made us think is that Sacral response is a one-dimensional sound. It has taken out gut feeling and everything that comes with that. Human Design explains Sacral response as a mechanical instrument that turns on or off with yes and no, and what we are forgetting is that behind a yes and a no is power and layers of guttural yeses and layers of guttural noes. As people that come from cultures that feel deeply, we have greater access to this once we decondition and move away from the idea that the decision-making is a mental process. When connected to our womb power, no matter our gender, we access a power that has been denied us.

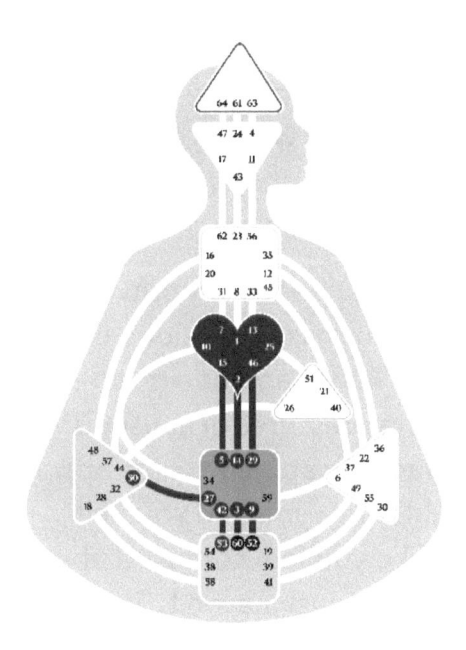

In modern-day society, logic and intellect are respected, and anything that defies the status quo is not. Society is trained to question anything that is not based in logic and when we have Sacral Authority, we find ourselves justifying our gut feelings. The challenge to overcome is to suspend the mind in moments when we are listening to the yes and no and fine-tuning the listening to hear the depth of feeling behind such responses. Although the mind is a tool to utilize, according to the Hindu chakra system, creative power is concentrated in the Sacral Center, and as a defined Sacral being you have a window into this consistent creative energy. The Sacral is orgasmic life force itself. When you honor your Sacral response, you lean into healing your own creative power.

For those with an *open* Sacral Center: you still have access to experimenting with amplifying this creative power when you are around Sacral Authority beings.

Emotional Authority

Emotional Authority is when you have a defined Solar Plexus Center, and this informs a wave of emotions that is a determining factor for making decisions.

In our society, Emotional Authority gets rushed and it doesn't allow you to make decisions that are in alignment with your desires, wants, and needs, so you can sometimes be at odds with the pressures of a rushed world. The rushed world is a product of capitalism and oppression. Often as an Emotional Authority, you find yourself in positions where other people make you feel confused about what you want but in actuality, you just haven't ridden your wave long enough. As an individual with Emotional Authority, you are not confused or indecisive, you are just unaware of how long it takes to for your emotional wave to bring clarity. The completion of the wave is the determining factor, and the flux of in-between emotions are the processing time.

That is where the work really is: discovering your wave.

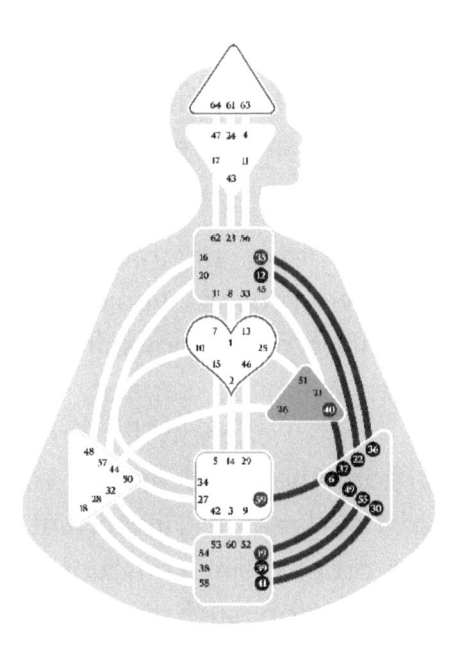

We talk about highs and lows in Human Design, but the exploration of your unique high and low is not commonly discussed. Depending on your experiences in the world, your highs can be anxiety-driven, and your lows can be trauma triggered, and if you are not aware of this, you believe you are indecisive. It is important as an Emotional Authority to monitor what you are actually feeling in all parts of your body as well as to allow space and time when it comes to making decisions as well, becoming an observer of how emotions affect the body, the thoughts, and awaiting the click of the yes and the click of the no. The click will feel neutral, clear, and unwavering. When you sense this, you know your wave is complete.

Capitalism and its effect on culture pressure you to think time is not yours but, the moment you are faced with a life-altering decision you deserve time and space to move through the emotional wave process. There are times when, as an individual with Emotional Authority, you bypass what you are feeling due to cultural expectations placed on you. The conditioning and pressure of expectation can mask the ability to feel a range of emotions.

Depending on the level of trauma, your Emotional Authority can have two versions: you can be someone who is attuned to the range of emotions, from joy to anger, or someone who has a limited capacity to feel emotions. When there is a limited capacity for emotions, decision-making comes from the mind and is void of honoring feelings. In case of the latter, it is important for you to bring more grace to the process since emotions can be attached to several different factors such as past experiences. Pay attention to what is true and what is possibly a trigger. As BIPOC there is an added layer of awareness to be attuned to in order to utilize Emotional Authority at its highest capacity. This takes heightened inner work and somatic awareness so that you have a deep knowledge of how emotions affect you physically and mentally. This means being a student of your inner landscape is of the utmost priority.

The wave is not one-size-fits-all, emotions are nuanced and as BIPOC you have another layer that you have to include. This is a layer of healing, and once you overcome it you have an incredible connection to your emotions and can access realms of joy and profound wholeness. There is no joy greater than when BIPOC communities experience full liberation and unbound expression.

Splenic Authority

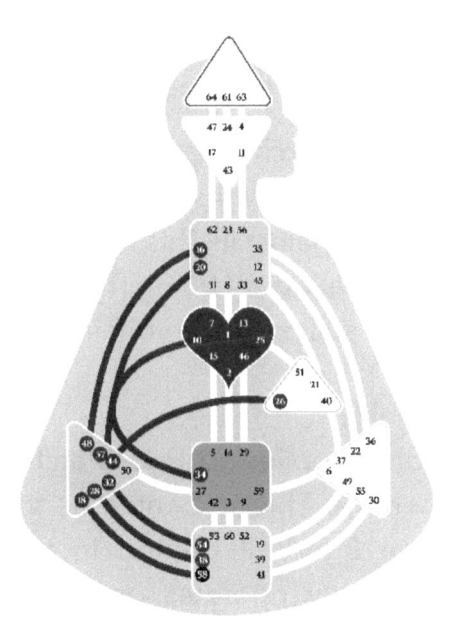

The Splenic Center is the communication center of the primal brain; therefore, survival, health, instinct, and intuition are influenced by this center. When tuned in, it is an unwavering knowing. The click of knowing is in the moment.

If you have Splenic Authority, you must foster trust in the moment and override excess mental dialogue. In life you are probably trained to value immediate positive results but in hindsight, you can see how a series of "wrong" turns lead to growth and blessings. You are most likely conditioned to avoid failure, yet the mystery of following your intuition leads you to results the mind cannot conjure. Life is a balancing act between honoring logic and intuition, but with Splenic Authority you are served by quieting the mind and learning to trust the mystery that resides in this center.

Past experiences affect this level of trust, and the proper healing of past failures frees you to know that life is always working for you; your mode of communication is through the unseen, loving forces that speak through the now.

Colonization and patriarchy may have robbed you of the inner knowing that comes with intuition and you have been taught to push back against it. This has caused you to stray away from your natural way of being. There is a way that you can utilize logic and still prioritize your intuitive intelligence.

Ego/Heart Authority

Ego Authority only applies to Ego Manifestors and Ego Projectors. Either the Throat Center or the G Center is connected to the Ego/Will Center. In textbook Human Design, Ego Authority operates on willpower and you either have it or you don't. However, the Ego is diminished because it is in reaction to something. As BIPOC you tend to either not have a sense of power, or power is in reaction to something.

The broken Will has the power to feel a personal strike very deeply and in turn, it vows to undo the broken. It is a cause and effect. When you have a defined Will Center, you have a process of going from victim to victorious and that lesson and process is locked in for you. The BIPOC experience is even more marked because of the revolutionary experiences life hands you day in and day out. As BIPOC you are engaged with the "opportunity" to explore your *will to overcome* constantly. Therefore, the Ego/Heart Authority for you as a BIPOC individual is a powerful Authority when channeled in an aligned place and when it has the space to truly heal the initial moment of breaking. Human Design states that the ego is led by the 45-21 Channel.

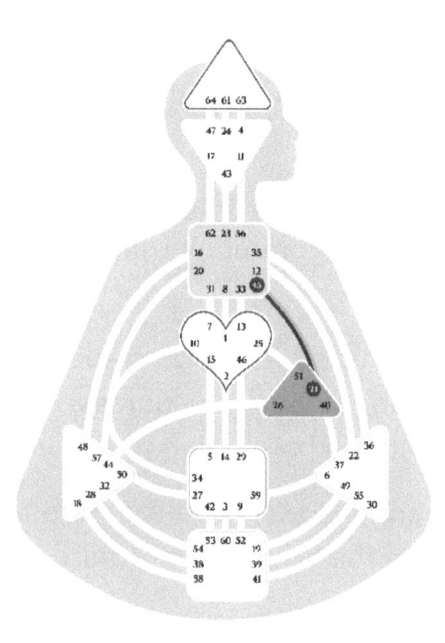

In order to understand the essence of this Authority, you have to dive into the channel. The power of the Will Center to mobilize and actualize energy is directly impacted by this channel for the community.

Gate 45 is about rulership, or someone able to rule or gather for the community. This natural Authority comes to teach or to bring for the good of all: *I have,* or *I haven't.* If you have Gate 45 and have not been put in a position of leadership or authority, you feel disempowered when not recognized, and feel okay to disengage. It is also possible with this gate you tend to not want to fight for your position. If you have to fight to be seen, it is deflating to your power and will. Gate 45 says *I know I am supposed to lead you, but I am not here to convince you I am the leader; let me lead or not.*

Gate 21 is the manager of resources, and this energy can come in extremes. You can either be oblivious to what you have to control as far as resources, or you are very detailed and meticulous in the management of resources. You can be materially independent but thrive and feel on purpose when given control.

Both of these gates are here to serve the personal, transpersonal, or universal community. In its highest expression, this channel is in service.

Channel 45/21 can both manage resources and also lead the dissemination of such resources. The direction of purpose is essential in harnessing the power of this energy.

If you have Channel 45/21, you are here to make money with the power of the Will, and it requires purpose to truly be actualized.

Self/Identity/G Center Authority

Self-Projected Authority is only for Projectors. It is composed of a connection from G Center to the Throat Center. This energy needs to see itself reflected on others, yet the clarity does not come from those receiving the information. With this Authority you need to hear yourself talk things through. The biggest issue as a BIPOC Self-Projector is that you don't feel heard, so it is challenging for you to use your authentic voice in moments of vulnerability. The energy of the G Center to the Throat Center is intrinsically vulnerable energy, as the G Center is deeply connected to identity.

Identity is threatened by the system because the system does not recognize the value of the person due to colonization; therefore, the tenderness and vulnerability of being, is further threatened. The connection points are specific through three channels: 7/31, 1/8, 13/33.

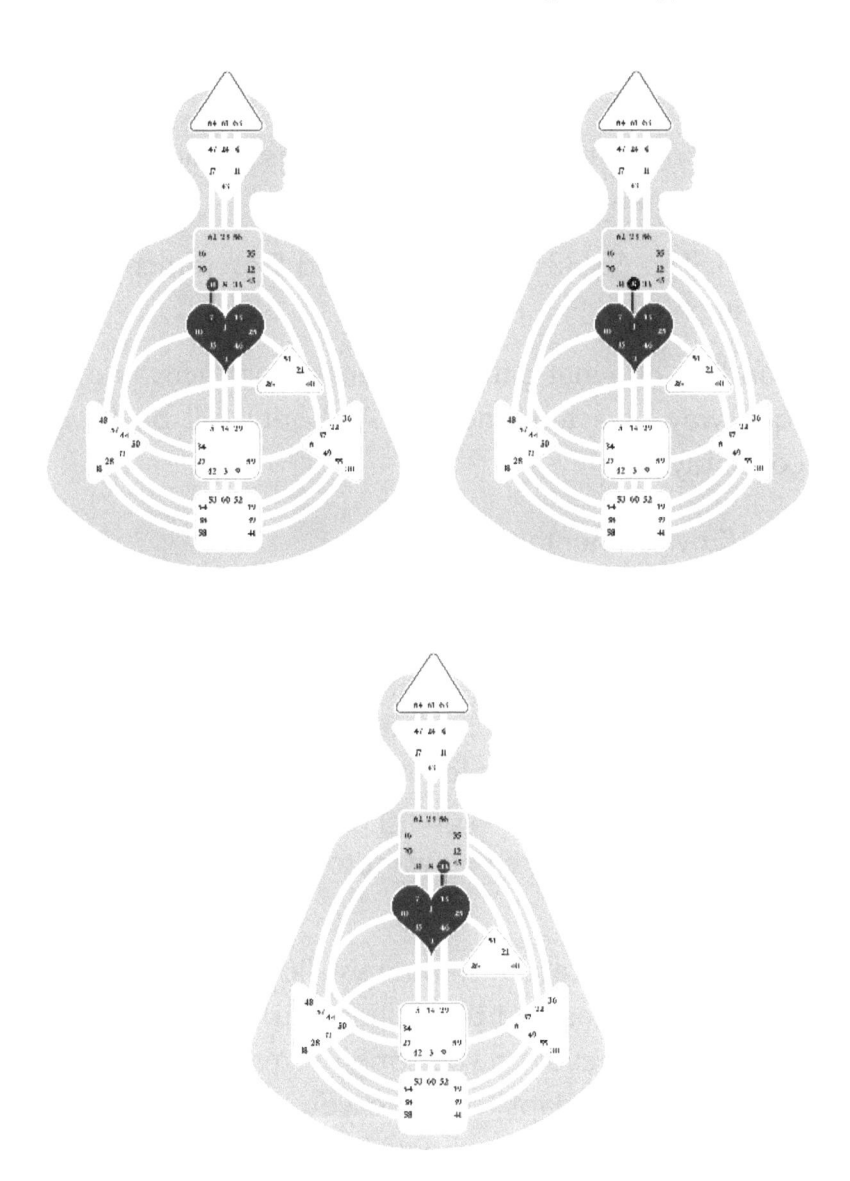

Let's examine the different voices of the Throat Center in *I lead* (Gate 31), *I know I can contribute* (Gate 8), *I remember* (Gate 33), and the effect of G Center through the roles of its gates: Projection and Logical Expression of the Self (Gate 7), Projection of Unique Creative Expression (Gate 1), and Reflection or Recording of the Past (Gate 13).

Democratic Leadership: The 7/31 Channel is a Democratic Appointment Leadership.

Unique Contribution: The 1/8 Channel is a Unique Creative Expression manifested as Purpose.

Prodigal: The 13/33 Channel is Lived Experience used as Wise Teachings.

Depending on what gates or channels are activated, your unique way of actualizing this Authority will be flavored accordingly.

Mental/Environmental Authority

As a Mental Authority, you are a Projector. And being in a space where you are listened to is the key. Being around people who want to influence their own agenda will not be helpful for you when verbalizing your process. The invitation is to seek people and environments that match where you want to go. It is going to be important to choose the environment where you want to be seen or wish to be influenced by.

For instance, if you are an immigrant, how can you integrate cultural differences and the values you align with without losing the connection to your origins? You can love where you come from, adapt to where you are, and make new roads expressing your authenticity within all communities that you identify with.

Similarly, if you come from a lower-income household, receiving education and career opportunities may feel contradictory and you will have to choose the value of the space that matches where you want to go.

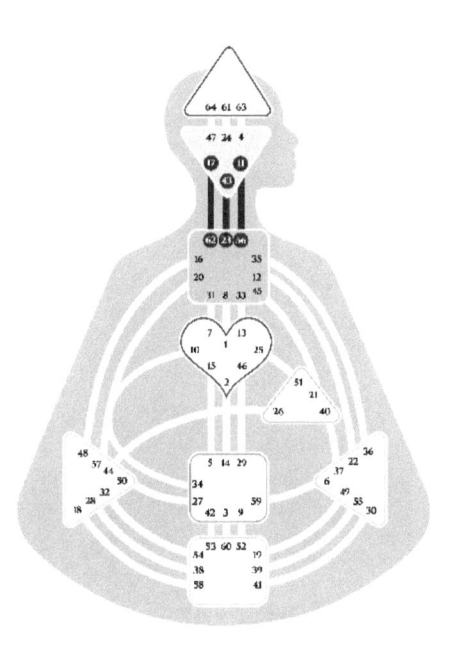

Mental and Environmental Projector role models are important for BIPOC, especially those that give you space to talk through your thoughts and provide feedback that encourages your own wisdom. It is important to seek mentors who offer that space, at various stages of your life. This doesn't mean that you are looking for people to mimic or mirror, but rather people you respect and who offer an elevated perspective. Exploring environments and possibilities beyond your culture or family of origin allows you to step into a synthesis of opportunities that match with people who are outside your usual social and economic status should this be important to you. And is not limited to material success: It is a compass guide for where you, as a Mental Projector, wish to be whether spiritual, emotional, etc. When you put your focus on envisioning and imagining the environments that light you up, you open yourself up creatively.

Your Soul Map

Lunar Authority

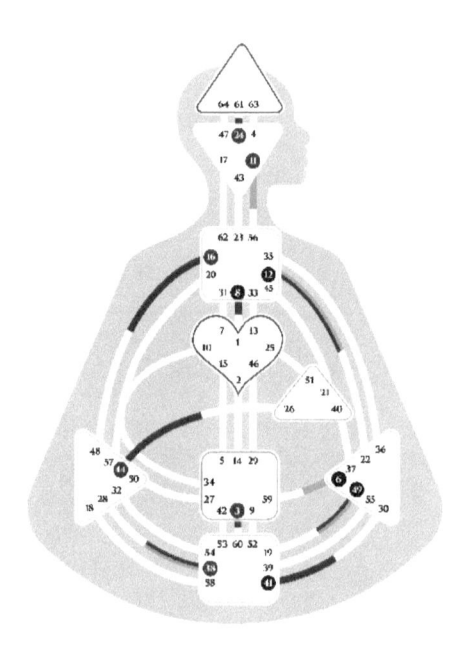

As a Reflector, when you are thriving and are happy at your job, the environment makes the experience. The environment you work in and engage with is imperative. If you don't have a job or career you love, you will find it challenging to thrive. As a Reflector, you have an overwhelming sense of service to humanity and that's why the right career is so enveloping for you. Allowing yourself to flow through the full Lunar cycle and its transits and reflecting upon the choices you are faced with when the cycle is complete, is how you make the right decisions. You know that when you have decided, it is a finite decision. The world is not set up for Reflectors to be given the amount of time needed to come to a conclusion. You must get into the habit of negotiating space and time to sort through all the variables, accompanied by the transits, so you can arrive at the click of certainty in the twenty-eight-day cycle. Just like the wave of the Emotional Authority, this click is an inner knowing that is locked in once the cycle is complete. Giving yourself the time is essential and it is important to not be too hard on yourself.

You may feel the added stress and pressure of negotiating and advocating as BIPOC, leading you to make decisions on job offers, for instance, without a sense of right timing and alignment. However, it is important that you find a way to honor yourself and the cycle that is so imperative to your well-being.

Definition: A Means to Empowerment

In the beginning there were no Types, but rather *definition* was the principal lens by which Ra interpreted individual charts. In Human Design your definition is what is consistent in you and what you can rely on. It creates your Type and determines your Strategy and Authority. But most importantly your definition determines how energy flows through you and how you take in energy in the world. These energetic connections allow you to connect with your communities, bond with others, and interconnect with the world as a whole.

1. No definition
2. Single definition
3. Split definition
4. Triple split definition
5. Quad split definition

Definition

In Human Design, definition refers to our defined channels and defined centers and how they are connected to each other. There are five types of definition: *no* definition, *single* definition, *split* definition, *triple split* definition, and *quad split* definition. We can think about definition as our personal operating system, like an inner language.

This is how we communicate, how we take in energy, and how we process information to arrive at intrinsic peace within ourselves. This defines the way in which we contemplate and come to conclusions. Having clarity soothes our nervous system, so understanding our definition is a nuanced way to feel aligned. It is important for us to do our best to follow and stay in alignment with our definition because it facilitates devotion to our Strategy and Authority.

It is of interest for each of us to have awareness of both our tropical and sidereal charts to begin to study the differences between them and see the correctness of each and how they are represented in our inner and outer realities.

No Definition

You are a Reflector. You have no defined centers; they are completely open. As a Reflector, it is about having conversations with trusted people who will facilitate a dialogue in which you can hear and sense yourself. The level of trust determines the precision and elevated space for the unfoldment of clarity.

Single Definition

In single definition all your defined centers are interconnected, making it one operating system. With that operating system there is a natural tendency for processes to happen on their own. It looks as though you, with single definition, don't need anyone, but what is happening is that you have your own way of working through the details to come to clarity. Getting to know this self-operating system is important because it is a finite destination. Once you are clear you can properly use Strategy and Authority.

Split Definition

There are two categories: *small split* and *large split*. A split definition means there are two operating systems (two individual groups of connected centers) that are not connected and therefore running independently. A small split needs a single gate to connect two defined circuits, a large split needs a full channel to connect two defined circuits. With split definition, you may feel the need to talk things through with someone as this is helpful to see your truth with the clarity of conscious dialogue.

Triple Split Definition

A triple split has three operating systems (three individual groups of connected centers) that are not connected so it needs a bridge to communicate and depending on your circuitry, you may need more than one. If one person completes your circuitry with their gates, that one person may be all you need.

Quadruple (Quad) Split Definition

The quad split may have either eight or all nine centers defined, but there will be gaps in connecting the centers. Based on *The Definitive Book of Human Design* by Lynda Bunnell and Ra Uru Hu, you as a quad split may have a slow lag time in resolution due to your inflexibility. It is recommended that you give yourself time and space and not subscribe to another's pressure in timing.

Profiles and I Ching

Your Profile is *how* you execute your Strategy and the role you came here to play. It comes from the I Ching and plays into understanding your place in humanity based on the Cosmos, utilizing the elements of yin and yang. Yin is the more Lunar, receptive elements, and yang is the more Solar, action elements; the interplay of both is what describes how nature and our lives move.

The I Ching consists of sixty-four trigrams that are constructed by six lines; the top three are called the *upper* trigram, and the lower three are called the *lower* trigram. The upper trigram is interpersonal, meaning it is in relation to others and is made up of Lines 6, 5, and 4. The lower trigram is personal, meaning it is in relation to self and is made up of Lines 3, 2, and 1.

Each line has an association with the upper or lower trigram. The upper trigram: Line 6, the Role Model, Line 5, the Heretic/Teacher, Line 4, the Opportunist/Networker.

The lower trigram: Line 3, the Martyr/Experimenter, Line 2, the Hermit/Introvert, Line 1, the Investigator.

There are two ways to determine your Profile; one is to look at the Human Design chart and the other is to pull the information from the conscious and unconscious Sun and Earth. There are twelve Profiles, or how's of the unfoldment of ourselves. The first number is based on the conscious aspect of the chart (black/Personality), or known personality, and the second number is based on the unconscious aspect of the chart (red/Design), and reflects the change, embodiment, and growth available for you.

The Profiles are extracted from looking at the lines in the conscious Sun and Earth (Personality) and unconscious Sun and Earth (Design).

The Profile comes from the decimals behind the gates.

Example: the conscious Sun (Personality) is in 14.4 and conscious Earth in 8.4.

The unconscious Sun (Design) is in 55.1 and the unconscious Earth in 59.1. This brings the Profile to 4/1, the 4-Line being the conscious Sun and Earth, and the 1-Line being the unconscious Sun and Earth.

Evolution of the Lines

Right Angle Profiles

Right Angle Profiles consist of 1/3, 1/4, 2/4, 2/5, 3/5, 3/6. Having a Right Angle Profile means that you are here to fulfill a personal destiny; you are here to awaken and live out your personal truth. You are here to focus on your soul curriculum primarily. In some ways these Profiles can seem selfish, but here is a reminder to refocus on your personal journey.

1/3 Profile

The 1/3 has the foundational aspect of the 1st Line (the Investigator) and the changing and evolving aspect of the 3rd Line (the Experimenter). You are the type of person that seeks information first and explores this information in real life, to then inform others of what you have found out. This Profile is said to not ever make "mistakes" because your learning process is central to living your purpose, especially in service to others. The 1st Line settles when it has information, and the 3rd Line feels complete when it explores the information. As a 1/3 Profile your drastic experimentation reveals truth and wisdom about your next steps, and by the time you are forty years of age, the wisdom from this lived experience becomes the knowledge and wisdom shared.

1/4 Profile

This Profile investigates first and enjoys information as a foundation. The growth of your 4th Line lies in exploring relationships and utilizing your network for evolution; you are one that feels comfortable moving on after the next step or foundation is in place. You can be more consciously focused inward and then utilize the exploration of your 1st Line to share with others afterward, through the 4th Line.

2/4 Profile

The 2/4 has a conundrum in relationship to others. The 2nd Line brings you to your own internal world (alone time) and is then magnetized out of hiding by others. The 4th Line is growth in how to utilize the power of networks. As a 2/4 you are very gifted in attracting opportunities, even though you do not want to be noticed. The timing of your readiness and willingness to be available is important, while still honoring the richness of your alone time.

2/5 Profile

This Profile has the dance of being seen, or not. There is a double magnetism to this Profile. Your 2nd Line needs alone time and draws magnetism from others as you are in a period of withdrawal, but the downtime is mostly needed for integrating information. There is a readiness required for your 2nd Line to come out. Your 5th Line and its projections (inspiration or triggering by others) requires you to really know your own timing and also avoid seeking approval from others so that the wisdom of your 5th Line can teach. Being alone provides you with a sense of safety. Ideally you are in a community that accepts and fully sees you.

3/5 Profile

This Profile is a risk taker and problem solver. The 3rd Line is the conscious action of trying new things, while the unconscious 5th Line is the growth of knowing that this is not about approval but in many ways of modeling so others can follow. As a 5th Line, you can have a need to be the knower of all things before speaking truth, but your 3rd Line requires a pause for the synthesis of experiences. You would best be served to worry less about what others think because people either will be inspired or affected in unconscious ways by your aura. People either like you or they don't and that is okay. The 5th Line has a destined path of being a teacher who cannot worry about what others think otherwise it will slow you down.

3/6 Profile

This Profile is very dynamic. You experiment due to your 3rd Line and have phases due to your 6th Line (see 4/6 Profile). At times you are unclear if you are experimenting or if you are going through a phase and the only way to decipher this is by getting to understand yourself over time; some might say that until the age of twenty-eight you are mostly 3rd Line and then the Role Model 6th Line comes into play after you are forty-eight years old. This Profile can feel like life is about struggle, but what you have to remember is that your accomplishments can be delayed, and your path is one of persevering, learning, and then coming into teaching after all you have learned.

4/6 Profile

The energy of the 4th Line draws people in, and the 6th Line has life stages. The 4th Line is the conscious aspect that pulls you into the complexity and richness of relationships. The 6th Line has three phases. Phase one, 0-28 years of age, is the *experimenting* phase. Phase two, 28-48 years of age, is the "on the roof" phase; this is the place of observing and learning how to do life and business. Phase three, post forty-eight years of age, is the embodiment and accomplishment of the Role Model, which you learn over time. Your 6th Line feels this destined path from a young age.

4/1 Juxtaposition

The dharmic path of this Profile is one of influencing the direction of the life curriculum. Your conscious path of relationships is foundational to your Profile while the 1st Line allows for curiosity and investigation to be the mode of learning. Your self-worth could determine the quality of your network and information. Therefore, it is important for you as a 4th Line to consciously choose a network of friends and colleagues that reflect the types of opportunities you desire. This can seem calculated, but it is the way to honor the magnetism of your incarnation.

Left Angle Profiles

Left Angle Profiles consist of 5/1, 5/2, 6/2, 6/3. The Left Angle (or transpersonal) Profiles are here to play out their life curriculum with others. These Profiles fulfill their dharmic path by engaging in relationships (romantic, platonic, and professional). We all need each other, but life pulls these Profiles to engage with others to fulfill their destiny. The conscious (first number) is a destiny path; of Teacher or Role Model, and the unconscious (second number) is the way the growth of this path will unfold. These Profiles feel from an early age that they are destined for something bigger than themselves, even if early in life these possibilities seem out of reach.

5/1 Profile

This Profile has an urge to serve the greater good but the projections (or agendas) of others influence you to a degree that if you do not know who you are, you can be steered down an inauthentic path. Your conscious 5th Line has a natural magnetism from others who project their needs onto you. Your 5th Line has to drop the approval of those around you and choose to connect with your truth and most authentic self. Your 1st Line leads you into a path of investigation and learning, which will be the foundation for how you lead. You are a magnetic leader, guided by your investigation to serve others, but in a bit of an impersonal way.

5/2 Profile

This Profile seems to have two sides to it; your 5th Line is genuinely interested in and intrigued by relationships and your 2nd Line does not want to be bothered. You feel pressure from the 5th Line to come out and speak and your 2nd Line has no desire to be seen. Because of this push and pull, it is up to you to motivate yourself to come out of the cave and teach and share; you have to want it. When you as a 5/2 come out to play, it is important that you know who you are. The projection or perception of others can trigger the wounds of the past. People can have a tendency to make the assumption that you as a 5/2 do not really know the core of who you are. You would benefit from having a community that accepts you fully.

6/2 Profile

This Profile has phases of being internal and external; based on your 2nd Line (introvert) and your readiness to be out, and also the three phases of your 6th Line (see the 4/6 Profile). The essence of a 2nd Line requires others to know how and when to draw you out in the world. The comfort zone of your alone time is a natural state of being until your destined Role Model phase (post forty-eight years of age) calls you out into the world. You can be resistant to that later stage in life, but the destiny of your 6th Line reminds you of the important work you are here to do in the world.

6/3 Profile

With this Profile you have the opportunity to use the wisdom you gather through the exploration that comes so natural to the 3rd Line, to support others. This will take time, and it is important to not get stuck in the pain and wounding of your story. Embrace your need to personally experience and experiment in life and understand that the lessons you learn along the way will bring wisdom and thrust you forward as a Role Model, once you come off the roof after the age of forty-eight. Use the time on the roof to heal and reflect on the lessons so you can come off empowered and ready to serve the world.

The Intersection of the Human Design Chart: Use It for Your Exaltation

Centers

We hear a lot about conditioning in Human Design, but for BIPOC our conditioning goes beyond the self; it is about an entire civilization that consciously or unconsciously requires us to stay in a specific condition so that the power remains in the status quo. Another factor is that there is a pervading perspective of openness and definition conditioning us to see our openness as flaws and our definition as strengths when in fact the nuanced gifts of each individual chart add flavor to the entire community. We are all conditioned to be shaped by a cookie-cutter model—for instance beauty, intelligence, gifts, personality, and various attributes—yet this model keeps us trapped in a standard that is inauthentic to our liberation.

Open Centers

Our greatest gifts lie in our openness; it is the place where Spirit can speak directly to us. These centers allow for the most profound themes in life to be explored, especially through interaction with others. Anywhere we have openness, the energy has an opportunity to be amplified through open-ended forms of communication, including the transits and those we are in community with (who have definition in these centers).

In many ways, our open centers are an invitation to acknowledge the pain and highlight the blessings.

Language matters, and in systems that help people better understand themselves, we must consider oppressive versus liberating language. In the case of centers, students and clients have informed us that the language used to describe the consistency of the centers is confusing and it makes them feel less than. In Traditional Human Design the terms *defined*, *undefined*, and *open* are used. The use of undefined can be perceived as disempowering language. Definition refers to everything that is colored in in the chart and where we have consistent energy. When we have a center that is undefined it is white with "hanging" gates, and an open center is completely disconnected from other centers. Both undefined and open centers amplify the energy of others and the environment. We would like to consider different terminology such as defined, open, and completely open centers as alternatives to traditional definitions.

Sahasrara (Head) Center

With an open Head Center, you are open to inspiration from all sources, areas, and modes. It is important for you to have a method of meditation or silencing of the mind to distinguish what thoughts are your own inspiration, and what thoughts and questions come from others. When you have an open Head, you experience an energetic exchange with those around you, or even the collective; this exchange translates into receiving the questions they have, and you may feel pressure to answer these questions. You tend to be very philosophical and have numerous questions swirling around you. If you have an open Head Center your goal is to be perceptive to information and not claim it as your own unless it truly resonates with you.

Agya (Ajna) Center

The Ajna Center is the place that synthesizes the questions and inspiration that come from the Head Center. With an open Ajna you are very open-minded and feel the freedom to play with different perspectives, including a genuine ability to have different ways of viewing one thing. If you have an open Ajna, you may feel pressure to materialize all your inspirations. Allow the ideas to flow and catch the ones that are most aligned.

Vishuddi (Throat) Center

The Throat Center is considered a place of manifestation. There is a misperception that those with open Throat Center have a challenge manifesting; however, that is not true. With an open Throat Center, you should more consciously choose the words you speak. This way you will not strain the physical and energetic voice and it will have the highest impact on others.

The refinement and timing of your energy and words are the most important thing to consider; ensure that those around you are the correct people to receive the truth.

Higher Anahata (Identity/ G) Center

The G Center is a part of the heart chakra and because the Magnetic Monopole resides here (a one-sided magnet that only attracts and is believed to be placed in the G Center at the time of conception), it is a center that determines much of our essence.

If you have an open G Center, you are here to be a student of your sense of identity. You have the ability to be a chameleon, but this does not mean you do not know who you are or what you want. Rather, you are intended to explore all the possibilities of identity available through people, experiences, and places. Be okay with being influenced by others but be mindful of how your network is composed. How you feel in your environment is extremely important and nourishes your thriving.

Lower Anahata (Will) Center

The Will Center is the energy of value, worth, and willpower. Having an open Will Center means that this is a central theme in life, especially in this modern capitalist world. If you have this center open, you have to learn how value plays a part in your life in order for you to heal your heart. Learning to experience your own value and worth from the inside out is the path of this center. Know that the willpower theme does not always resonate because as

BIPOC you may push through your exhaustion to survive. Rest, as a revolutionary choice, must be honored. Also, acknowledge the extra taxing circumstances in which you live. Because of modern times, this is an area where extra support, coaching, and mentorship could well serve you.

Manipura (Spleen) Center

This center is the center for instinct and survival. Openness here becomes an exploration of your fears and what it is you need to be truly safe. This center is associated with the reptilian brain and animalistic survival, meaning that fears may be perceived as an immediate threat. Pay attention to the information that comes to you and move through it using your personal Strategy.

It is important for you to establish boundaries to protect your peace and develop your intuitive and instinctual awareness. Honing this skill set will protect you from amplifying the fears of those around you and knowing when you are safe and when you are not safe.

Manipura (Emotional Solar Plexus or Solar Plexus) Center

This is the center for emotion. Openness here is the marker for the empath, the one who feels everything around them—the people and the collective. If you have an open Solar Plexus, it can bring about a feeling of instability, but really it is your greatest gift. What you feel is not necessarily all yours and even though you do have a hook to all that you experience, it is about learning to let emotions pass through you. You crave harmony and you want to mend anything that interferes with that. Focus on strong emotional boundaries, knowing what is yours and what is not. Grounding and meditation are important so that you can differentiate yourself from others.

Swadhisthana (Sacral) Center

The Sacral Center is the center of work energy and sexual energy. In the Hindu chakra system, this is the creative center and works less on mechanics and more on flow, creativity, sound, and tone. If you have an open Sacral Center, it requires you to monitor your energetic input and output, who you are around, and what environments affect you; this is not to control it but to have awareness of your body. Having an open Sacral does not mean you don't have energy, it means that your energy supply is either limited or in waves of abundance, depending on circumstances. When you are in tune with your body you know exactly how much energy to put into situations, people, and projects. With an open Sacral, you can have unlimited energy when you are turned on by other people's lives and creative ventures. You can be in energetic flow by putting yourself in environments that are positive and have a reciprocal energetic exchange; therefore, plan accordingly for your seasons of availability.

Muladhara (Root) Center

This is the center for timing, including divine timing. Openness can feel like pressure to do—the never-ending to-do list. This openness allows you to produce at high levels but be mindful that your liberation and freedom are not bought by how much work you do. You are free, whether work gets done or not. Having an open Root Center is really about finding your own pace instead of giving in to the pace of society. Having an open Root Center can cause you to amplify other people's stress and pressure to do.

Defined Centers

Defined centers can be an anchor and stabilizing energy once you get to know the different aspects of yourself and how each of the centers express that. Consistency in inspiration (Head) is vastly different from consistency in voice (Throat). Even though your definition grounds you in your beliefs, it's important to leave room for changing thoughts, views, and opinions. And when that change happens, to not feel that your identity is being compromised. It can be hard to pivot into a new season of different consistent energy. The overall theme is that in many ways consistency is relaxing to our nervous system because those elements feel more predictable.

Sahasrara (Head) Center

Having a defined Head Center means you have a pre-scripted or consistent way of receiving information. Meaning, if you receive information through one source you will always receive it that way. It's important to pay attention to the gates you have active to know when that inspiration hits you. You can receive this information through doubt (Gate 63), knowing (Gate 61), or confusion/downloads (Gate 64). It's important for you to tune into the easiest and most consistent way to receive information.

Agya (Ajna) Center

This center is for processing inspiration and making it into a synthesis and language of sorts. When you have definition here, you tend to have truth locked in and this, although compelling, can make you a bit stubborn and can inhibit you to see other people's points of view and potentially have conflictive relationships. It's important for you to remember that the way you see things is *one* possibility, and only one. However, the way you process information and are able to organize it can be so helpful to those who can align with your lens; just ensure that you leave room for others to dialogue.

Vishuddi (Throat) Center

With this center it's important to know its connection to the other centers. Where the connection is, that is where you will have consistent energy to the throat. For instance, if you have a connection from the Ajna to the Throat, your thoughts can be easily communicated. If you have a connection from the Throat to the G Center, the essence of the gate in the G Center will be easily yet tenderly communicated. Having a defined Throat also holds a frequency that people resonate with, and they therefore recognize the message quicker. Know that what you say is compelling to others.

Higher Anahata (Identity/G) Center

The G Center is the center of identity and direction. When you set out on a path or goal or have been taught a specific identity, the pivot to re-inventing yourself or going in a new direction can be challenging. You can change direction, but your thoughts, ideas, and tendencies of who you are can crush your world when you are so attached to your persona. However, the conviction in self is so strong and inspiring, it allows others to find their own direction. Pay attention to the highlighted gates, as that is the way in which you channel this divine-led direction.

Lower Anahata (Will) Center

This center is the placement of value and the tenacity to accomplish a vision. There is a tendency for your words and actions to come across as pompous and arrogant, but this is actually your confidence and ability to execute. Once you overcome narratives around value, you lock it into place within you, and your presence activates others to fulfill what they wish to accomplish. It is important that you give yourself time to rest and regenerate. It is also important that you are careful how you impose your will on others because if they have an open Will Center, they cannot exert things into being. You will want to be conscious of your force and compassionate to the experience of others when it comes to their ever-changing sense of value and will.

Manipura (Spleen) Center

This is the center for animalistic instinct. As BIPOC and the way you were raised and conditioned, you have to decipher what is fear-based and what is your intuition. To distinguish this, it is important for you to know that intuition is silent and calm, and fear is loud. Having a defined Spleen can sometimes cause doubt; you may sense a blind spot. Your intuitive hits are quick and spot on, but you can tend to overlook them. You doubt yourself because of the past, and you can tend to hold on to the past and ignore your brilliance overriding your intuitive hits. You know your aligned path based on your intuitive feeling; don't ignore it.

Manipura (Emotional Solar Plexus or Solar Plexus) Center

This powerful center and the exploration of emotional waves offer you so much. You can confuse this energy as "being too sensitive" and it is important that you know this definition allows you to feel a whole range of emotions. Release those emotions out of your body in the most aligned way—crying or through movement, for example. You cannot stop the wave. Do not make decisions when you are in the midst of the wave; what you feel in one moment will change once you have ridden this wave. The waves can be minutes, days, weeks, or even months, and becoming your own detective to better understand your waves is encouraged. Paying attention to the defined channel(s) and gates is a good way to better understand the waves: the community wave (known as tribal), the individual wave, and the collective wave.

Swadhisthana (Sacral) Center

This is the center for energy, work, and pleasure. The Sacral hums and it is driven by sounds and vibrations within the body. Traditionally, in Human Design, the teachings have instructed you to be connected to your yes and no via the sounds uh-huh (yes) and uh-uh (no), but rarely is the tone of your yes and no explored. The Sacral Center, also known as the *womb center* (or *dan tien* in traditional Chinese medicine) is the embodiment of pleasure and it exudes power when it is turned on. In our culture, you have not been encouraged to prioritize pleasure, power, and the unlimited energy that comes from this natural state. The womb center is not only for female-identifying humans. All people have access to the universal life force expressed in this center.

Muladhara (Root) Center

This grounding center is about adrenalized pressure. Definition here allows you to manage stress and it allows you to manage yourself. Complete channels from the Root to the Sacral is a marker for having on and off switches; honor those and know that all will get done in divine timing. The defined Root Center gives you your own rhythm and pressure from the outside world is not yours; you march to the beat of your own drum.

Gates

Gates in Human Design correlate to a hexagram of the I Ching. Each gate is represented by an astrological sign, a Human Design center, a part of the body, and makes up one part of a channel, which is created when two gates are connected.

Conscious Gates

Consciousness in the chart is defined by the right-hand column [your Personality] with black numbers that correlate to the black lines in the chart. It is the energy that you have had access to since the beginning of this lifetime. It is the aspect of yourself that is obvious to you and that expresses your dharma (your soul's purpose).

Unconscious Gates

These are the gates expressed in the left-hand column of your chart with red numbers that correlate to the red lines. The unconscious gates are what your soul wants you to learn in this lifetime; they are less obvious in youth and become more entrenched as you mature. Knowing your soul path creates a journey that is more harmonious. When you don't know your Design curriculum, life feels more challenging.

Conscious, Unconscious, and Repetition

When you have the same gate both conscious and unconscious, at different points in your life you will experience both expressions. Some aspects will feel like pieces you embody, and others will feel like there is a learning and deepening with it. It is important to note the planetary location of the gate.

When a gate is repeated in different planets, there is an invitation to pay attention to this energy and explore the accent of this gate.

Keynote of Gates

The unconscious and conscious aspects of the gates express through us. Having an understanding of the potential of a gate and what is unconscious is the first step in embodying the high expression.

Let's remember that the synthesis of the gates is an essence we are attempting to grasp from the original stories of the hexagrams in the I Ching. We recommend you take the time to read the stories of the I Ching to have a somatic experience and integration of each of the hexagrams (a.k.a. the gates).

The *keynote*[58] is a word or phrase describing how energy is expressed.

- High expression—the highest level of potential.
- Low expression—the unregulated unconscious.

---

[58] Credited to Karen Curry Parker. Some of the keynotes used in this section are from the Quantum Human Design™ system.

Gate 1–Creativity

High expression–Beauty in all things

Low expression–Frenetic anxiety

Gate 2–Receive Support

High expression–Universal support

Low expression–Taking advantage

Gate 3–Innovation

High expression–Allowing synthesis

Low expression–Having a hard time starting

Gate 4–Mental Solutions

High expression–Universal knowing

Low expression–Apathy and frustration

Gate 5–Universal Timing

High expression–Surrendering to time

Low expression–Controlling timing

Gate 6–Emotional Balance

High expression–Truth and diplomacy

Low expression–Emotionally judgmental

Gate 7–Leadership Support

High expression–Empowered leadership

Low expression–Stubborn

Gate 8–Contribution

High expression–Refined role model

Low expression–Inauthentic voice

Gate 9–Focus

High expression–Aligned focus

Low expression–Undisciplined energy

Gate 10–Self-Love

High expression–Understanding of love of self and others

Low expression–Victim

Gate 11–Ideas

High expression–Divine inspiration

Low expression–Fear of ideas not heard or expressed

Gate 12–Romantic

High expression–Allowing romance in all things

Low expression–Overly cautious, unclear and untrusting

Gate 13–The Listener

High expression–Natural witness

Low expression–Overly fixating on the past

Gate 14–Prosperity

High expression–Provisioned to overflow

Low expression–Getting stuck doing something for money

Gate 15–Love of Humanity

High expression–Magnetism for the collective

Low expression–Self-sacrificing

Gate 16–Enthusiasm

High expression–Versatile talent

Low expression–Feeling talentless

Gate 17–Opinions

High expression–Mature awareness of possibilities

Low expression–Opinionated and enforcing opinions on others

Gate 18–Improving

High expression–Ability to course correct toward joy

Low expression–Perfectionist or critically compromising

Gate 19–Connected

High expression–Unwavering connection to all things

Low expression–Emotionally demanding

Gate 20–Anticipation

High expression–Presence

Low expression–Impatience

Gate 21–Management/Control

High expression–Conscious accounting

Low expression—Micromanaging and fear of being controlled

Gate 22—Grace

High expression—Royal graciousness

Low expression—Inappropriate expression

Gate 23—Explanation

High expression—Succinct synthesis

Low expression—Fragmented thinking

Gate 24—Rationalizing

High expression—Devoted processing

Low expression—Anxious thoughts

Gate 25—Acceptance

High expression—Unconditional love

Low expression—Feeling insignificant

Gate 26—Accumulation

High expression—Integrous vision

Low expression—Covert manipulation

Gate 27—Nourishing

High expression—Compassionate caring

Low expression—Self-sacrifice and codependency

Gate 28–Tenacity

High expression–Knowing and discernment of what is worth the effort, and what is not

Low expression–Fear of a purposeless life accompanied by struggle

Gate 29–Commitment

High expression–Devotion

Low expression–Over-committing

Gate 30–Intensity

High expression–Passionate pursuits

Low expression–Boredom in the mundane

Gate 31–Influence

High expression–Unexpected anointed leadership

Low expression–Forceful power

Gate 32–Endurance

High expression–Steady movement toward that which is valued

Low expression–Fear of failure and doubt in vision

Gate 33–Storyteller

High expression–Ability to speak your truth

Low expression–Forgetting and disacknowledgment of the past

Gate 34–Power

High expression–Commanding presence

Low expression–Extremes of either passive or pushy

Gate 35–Aptitude/Progress

High expression–Adventure that moves something bigger forward

Low expression–Either jaded or afraid to be rejected

Gate 36–Adventure

High expression–Passionate, sexual and emotional adventure, having incorporated lessons from the past

Low expression–Leaping into things without self-regulation

Gate 37–Harmony

High expression–Communicating what is needed to arrive at peace

Low expression–Inability to communicate needs and a lack of patience in the process to arrive at peace and harmony

Gate 38–Fight for Right

High expression–Purposeful direction

Low expression–Unwavering stubborn direction

Gate 39–Activist/Provocation

High expression–Sacred provocation with a receptive audience

Low expression–Unconscious provocation without the lens of impact

Gate 40–Effective/Deliverance

High expression–The will to provide for a community

Low expression–Overextending the self without boundaries and a lack of belongingness

Gate 41–Imagination

High expression–Dreaming on endless possibilities

Low expression–Delusional fantasy or repressed desires

Gate 42–Completion

High expression–Aligned plan with intent to complete, and open to new cycles

Low expression–Feeling and acting on the pressure to finish

Gate 43–Breakthrough

High expression–Knowing, insight, and correct timing of new ways of doing things

Low expression–Either blurting things out or holding back in fear of being rejected

Gate 44–Patterns

High expression–Leaning into the ability to know patterns and prepare others for what's next

Low expression–Suspicious

Gate 45–CEO/Chief Executive/Queen

High expression–Benevolent leader focused on the wealth of the community

Low expression–Uncomfortable with leading

Gate 46–Loving Embodiment

High expression–Sensual vitality

Low expression–Disconnected from the body

Gate 47–Epiphany

High expression–Positive mindset and trusting the process

Low expression–Stuck in trying to "figure it out"

Gate 48–Depth/Fresh Knowledge

High expression–Knowing when you have enough wisdom

Low expression–Inaction due to feeling inadequate or blindly seeking wisdom

Gate 49–Wisdom/Revolution

High expression–Wisdom in the life cycle of a partnership

Low expression–Afraid to be in partnership or rejecting others without analyzing

Gate 50–Values

High expression–Maternal high values for the community

Low expression–Sacrificial for the benefit of the community

Gate 51–Arousing

High expression–Initiate for the love of Spirit and toward a bigger picture

Low expression–Shocking for the sake of shock

Gate 52–Perspective

High expression–Stillness in contemplating

Low expression–Unfocused energy

Gate 53–The Starter

High expression–Aligned beginnings that manifest through Strategy and Authority, without the need to finish

Low expression–Finishing things that no longer interest or not starting due to self-doubt

Gate 54–Ambition

High expression–Chief dreamer of any project or venture in spaces that give recognition

Low expression–Unconscious ambition for malicious gain

Gate 55–Abundance

High expression–Unwavering trust in Spirit

Low expression–Feeling lack and limited

Gate 56–Seeker/Wanderer

High expression–Using stories to stimulate expansive ideas in others

Low expression–Telling stories with no objective

Gate 57–Intuition

High expression–Clairaudience that is acted upon

Low expression–Ignoring intuition

Gate 58–Joy

High expression–Maintaining a vision of what joy is

Low expression–Unsatisfied with life and feeling pressure to be of service

Gate 59–Intimacy

High expression–An ability to go deep in relationships and experience sexual intimacy if desired

Low expression–Going deep with the wrong people or not establishing intimate boundaries with others

Gate 60–Resourcefulness

High expression–The urge to create deliberate newness

Low expression–Unwillingness to change

Gate 61–Wonder

High expression–Trusting the inner knowing

Low expression–Trying to explain or make sense of the inner knowing

Gate 62–Planning

High expression–Tapping into the ability to sequence complex things

Low expression–Being confused and not tapping into the ability to sequence the details

Gate 63—Questioning

High expression—Critical thinkers; initiating hypothesis leading to possible solutions

Low expression—Self-doubt and worry

Gate 64—Big Picture

High expression—Allowing the vision to drop in, and patience in receiving the missing pieces of the puzzle

Low expression—Confusion and not trusting the process

The Channels (Simplified[59])

There are three main circuits (or combinations of channels) and they all have sub-circuits: individual circuitry group (knowing, centering, and integration circuit), collective circuitry group (sensing and understanding circuit), and community circuitry group (ego and defense circuit).

Individual Circuit Group

This carries individuation energy and focuses on inner change. This can be inspiring and work as a role model to others.

61/24 Channel of Awareness

Out-of-the-box big thinking that inspires and prompts others to consider life's mysteries

---

[59] credit: names from Traditional Human Design.

43/23 Channel of Structuring
Innovative thinking that improves and structures systems

1/8 Channel of Inspiration
Expressing unique creative energy that inspires others

2/14 Channel of The Alchemist
A strong auric field that empowers others and knows how to generate and manage resources

3/60 Channel of Mutation
Contributes new change in the world for others to grow and adapt

38/28 Channel of Struggle
Trailblazer energy that seeks to know what is worth the effort of commitment

39/55 Channel of Emoting
Radical acceptance of all emotions and the implementation of the creative energy that comes forth

22/12 Channel of Openness
Affects others through emotions and honors timing to move from rage to grace

57/20 Channel of the Brainwave
Trusting spontaneous in-the-moment intuition that is void of logic

34/20 Channel of Charisma
Inspires others with aliveness and enthusiasm for whatever it is they are responding to

10/20 Channel of Awakening

Impacting others by embodying the power that lies in loving one's inner essence

57/10 Channel of Perfected Form

Intuitive heartfelt guidance

57/34 Channel of Power

Moment-by-moment intuitive response in the now

25/51 Channel of Initiation

Abrupt encounters with Spirit through experiences that go beyond the comfort zone to push the boundaries of what is possible

34/10 Channel of Exploration

Focuses only on doing what they love and creating their own way

Community Circuitry Group

This relates to familial or close community dynamics.

21/45 Channel of Resources/ The Money Line

Independent enterprise and tendency to do all alone, ideally considering those impacted

44/26 Channel of Surrender

Magnetic staging to sell an idea or product

54/32 Channel of Ambition/Transformation

Holds the vision and does the work necessary to actualize success

19/49 Channel of Synthesis

A sensing-energy that is needed to bond in personal or business relationships

37/40 Channel of Community

Makes community agreements for the sake of creating a harmonious environment

27/50 Channel of Preservation

Maintains lineage and values for the community through nourishment

59/6 Channel of Mating

Holds the energy for birthing humans and projects

Collective Circuitry Group

This relates to the survival of humanity on a larger scale, i.e., organizations, governments, etc. This includes knowledge, logic, and experience of the whole.

63/4 Channel of Logic

Questions the logic of the status quo to arrive at an answer to a problem

17/62 Channel of Acceptance

Gathers fact and detail-driven knowledge

7/31 Channel of the Alpha

Democratic benevolent leadership that understands and uses patterns and trends to lead their communities

5/15 Channel of Rhythm
Honors the cycles and season and brings harmony to humanity

9/52 Channel of Concentration
Determined and sustainable focus that starts with stillness

18/58 Channel of Judgment
Critical thinking that improves systems for the good of all; the focus is on the systems and not on the self

48/16 Channel of the Wavelength
Passionately learns every aspect of something, arriving at mastery and then flowing with it

64/47 Channel of Abstraction
Initial confusion that leads to a journey of evolving philosophies in society

11/56 Channel of Curiosity
Curiously explores new ideas that in turn inspires great storytelling

13/33 Channel of the Prodigal
Retelling experiences and lessons of the past in a way that teaches others

29/46 Channel of Discovery
Fully embodied devotion that has definitive cycles without the expectation of specific results

53/42 Channel of Maturation
The ability to repeat cycles that bring wisdom over time

41/30 Channel of Recognition

Dreaming and feeling whether something leads somewhere or not, and the energy for tapping into the creation of new realities

35/36 Channel of Transitoriness

An adventurous exploration of life, meant to gather wisdom over time

Planets

The planets influence and inform how we play out the gates in our chart. Each gate is associated with a planet, and you may find that some gates repeat themselves in several different planets, which means that the theme of that gate is something to pay extra attention to and will express itself in a variety of ways. Each gate influences your life differently depending on the way the planet expresses itself through you. Knowing the energy corresponding to each planet is helpful in understanding the type of access you have for each gate.

Sun

The Sun expression is the gift you give to others: your personality, your gifts, your highest identity. In Human Design it is seen as the focal point, as everything in the chart works toward the fullest and highest expression of the conscious Sun Gate.

Earth

The Earth is what grounds you and what you receive from life.

Moon

The Moon is your intuitive, instinctive, and emotional wants, a driving force and a home for your heart.

North Node

The North Node is the direction your soul wants you to move toward in this lifetime. This is the opposite of your comfort zone. The themes of the North Node become more heightened the closer you get to the age of forty.

South Node

The South Node is the theme from your past lives; the things you will feel most comfortable doing.

☿

Mercury

Mercury is what you are here to communicate to the world; the thoughts and ideas you share and teach.

♀

Venus

Venus is your value system, what you love, and your relationship needs, wants, and desires. Venus shows what you exude and attract.

♂

Mars

Mars is the opportunity for growth, drive, and motivation, and your connection to the physical body. It can also be the area to mature into. Mars can be the indicator of what you are willing to fight for.

♃

Jupiter

Jupiter is the blessings and expansion planet. It is the connection to Spirit, your belief and faith, hopes and dreams. Jupiter holds the energy of the gifts and opportunities life brings us.

Saturn

Saturn keeps you in check; it is the steady step-by-step that encourages you to stay the course methodically. It has a maturation process, and as long as you follow its guidance, the path will be smooth.

Uranus

Uranus is how you are here to stand out; it is the unexpected plot twist in life at times. It is how you align with others; your inner humanitarian and it is generational.

Neptune

Neptune is your intuition and connection to Spirit, and it is the spiritual work and journey you are here to do. The work with Neptune involves the removal of illusions so you can arrive at truth.

Pluto

Pluto is about endings and beginnings; how you evolve and transform. Pluto represents what is expansive.

Chiron

Chiron is the Wounded Healer; it is the energy that beckons wholeness. The healing that allows you to then help others in that area.

Incarnation Cross

The Incarnation Cross is the combination of the conscious and unconscious Sun and Earth Gates. The Incarnation Cross is the strongest force within your chart and envelopes your life purpose themes. The combination of all four gates is the composite energy that becomes the theme of situations in your life; it draws people and opportunities to you related to its theme. When you are following your Strategy and Authority, your Incarnation Cross naturally unfolds. There is no need to seek it out or move toward it; it will be a part of you as you move through life in an aligned way.

Embodiment of Human Design

We all find Human Design at various points in our lives. It is important to factor in that we have experiences and knowledge of our life before Human Design, so we might have resistance to accepting the system because it is unfamiliar to us. It takes time and practice and trusting your Strategy and Authority to come to a place where you find yourself one step closer to feeling free to be yourself.

You are not lost. You have discovered a new part of yourself. Human Design can provide tools that make it possible to stay in alignment with what your soul has come here to do in this lifetime.

Ages and Stages of Human Design Discovery

The markers that determine the general seasons each human experiences are bookmarked by stages that align with the planet and developmental stages. Depending on your age when you enter into Human Design, there may be themes that are more prevalent.

Birth to Early Adulthood—0 to 17 Years

Think back and consider how you developed as a child. What was your environment like, your temperament, interests, and struggles? When it comes to your children, take note of their Strategy and their sensitivity with the open centers and potential dynamics with family and friends. The most important thing is to understand how your child develops: How they like to be in their environment, their temperament, interests, gifts amplified, and their struggles. The main thing as a parent is to note their Strategy, their sensitivity with the open centers, and the potential dynamics with family and friends.

For your young adults at home, it is important that their autonomy is allowed to be explored, and they need to know that they are encouraged to be their unique selves and to embrace their differences.

If you are currently in this phase, the biggest thing is to understand your uniqueness. It is about how you learn and how you develop your individuality and relationship dynamic with friends. This is extremely formative of how you will be as an adult.

Pre-Saturn Return Adults—18 Years to 27 Years

This is when you begin to feel empowered in taking ownership of your life. This is the time to explore, fail, succeed, and test all the possibilities in life while feeling that you have a soft place to land with those that love you.

First Saturn Return Adults—28 Years to 30 Years

If you are in your Saturn return, you may feel as though everything you have known is challenging your way of seeing, thinking, and doing things. You may find yourself switching career paths. This is a time when you can get clear about the next phase in your life. These are pivotal years to decide who you want to be.

Post Saturn Return Adults—31 Years to 39 Years

This is the time when you learn and observe life, and you establish your values. These years are the foundation of the school of life. There is a clarity that is presented to you that if you decide to choose yourself, life becomes smoother and sweeter. This establishes your personal brand.

North Nodes Adults—40 Years to 49 Years

This is the era of establishing the direction of those values in the sign and house of your North Nodes. The life themes embedded in your astrology and Human Design North Nodes become the focal point, should you want to co-create with life rather than force your personal agenda. This gives you the opportunity to embrace your truth; no need to pretend to make other people feel comfortable. This is a time to first explore the themes in your North Nodes and then once embodied, merge them with the gifts of your South Nodes.

Uranus Opposition–Around 41 Years to 47 Years

This is the beginning of what is known as the midlife crisis (or breakthrough); it is the shift out of the thirties, and themes are often around changing careers, ideas of what family means, and what you want to create, destroy, or build as a new foundation.

Chiron Adults–48 Years to 52 Years

This is a beautiful time to dial in the astrology and Human Design threads and do the final tweaks of alignment needed for you to continue the next level of your highest destiny. This is the prime of your life, ridden with midlife breakthroughs to encourage you to recognize how far you have come and reveal the subtle layers that still need to be addressed. It is the end of a cycle but also the start of a new empowered and liberated cycle.

Second Saturn Return Adults–56 Years to 62 Years

This time provides an opportunity to attain your dreams and plan the second half of your life.

Beyond 58 Years

This is the era of the sage; the wise teacher who has the ability to gather the lessons of the past, the wisdom of a life fully lived, and the energy of the one who can be available to live fully in their pleasure and calling and available to mentor others.

Bringing It All Together

For BIPOC it can feel as though the world is not meant for us, and although we have evidence to affirm this, we have another choice. Full liberation of our beauty and our birthright to thrive is what our ancestors are fueling for us. We are changing so many generational patterns and also remembering our ancestral connection to Earth and to Spirit. The remembering of our true essence is the exact curriculum we are being invited to participate in. Human Design is a tool—a tool that can give us a roadmap to heal and to work with universal laws with little resistance. Human Design is not a fix-all of generational trauma or the pain of our people; however, it can be a pathway to help us heal ourselves by giving us a way to find solutions in everyday life and providing a way to be in flow with ourselves and the world around us. Human Design can be the roadmap needed to flourish and thrive in our self-fulfillment, relationships, emotional wellness, career, finances, and spiritual well-being, as well as how we build harmonious communities.

For those of us with mixed ancestry, we hold so many identities within us. The way we feel inside sometimes invokes a sense of not belonging anywhere. Sometimes we hold the ancestral history and lineage of the oppressor and the oppressed, and it is through healing all the parts that we recognize that all parts of ourselves are worthy. We are living in a time when we would all be served to prioritize the voices of those most affected by colonization; this impacts the past, our families, and the current opportunities given by the world.

This book is meant to carve a safe space to introduce Human Design knowing its origins are questionable, knowing the community is primarily non-BIPOC, and *still* advocating for how we can use this potent tool to make it work for us. We are done making the world feel comfortable in our presence and we now claim to take up space in a way that is aligned, generous, and for the good of all.

Despite the evidence in the world that has pushed us to hide our Indigenous roots, we are worthy—worthy of being fully expressed in the world, worthy of having agency in our lives, despite what the world tells us, and worthy of wholeness in all our parts. As we allow ourselves to reclaim our power and our worthiness, we honor the challenges of our ancestors and seed the wholeness, the prosperity, and the abundance of the future generations.

Contributors from Our Interviews

We would like to thank the following contributors for their interviews: Clarinda Mann, Elmina Bell, Fiona Wong, Jasmine Nnenna, and Karen Curry Parker.

Clarinda Mann

I went through a major awakening experience in 2011, and it energetically pushed my life in a completely new direction. I became fascinated with esoteric knowledge, energy work, and astrology, and I knew that one day I would utilize my talents to help bring transformation to others. I was recently introduced to Human Design and have been amazed at the depth and accuracy of insight it has brought to my understanding of myself. I am committed to helping others learn more about their unique identity and bringing healing to areas of their life that require attention by showing them how Human Design and astrology can transform their perspective.

I know that we all have a unique purpose, and I strive to assist others to help go through their personal transformation in a safe and healthy way.

Over time, I have witnessed the power the planetary energies have on us here on Earth. My focus is on looking at the energies that each individual has in their Human Design and astrological charts to identify areas that are asking for healing in this lifetime.

I truly believe that everything we need to heal has been given to us like a guidebook. Human Design, astrology, and Reiki are powerful tools and have been given to us in these times to help us evolve as spiritual beings.

astroenergetics.org

Elmina Bell

Elmina Bell (she/they) hails from Indigenous African parents from the Indigenous Bantu Sawa/Subu peoples of Cameroon in Central Africa, and the Ewe peoples of Togo West Africa and was born and raised in Washington, DC (Indigenous Piscataway land). Elmina is a multiple neurodivergent/neuroexpansive person who centers Indigenous holistic psychologies and cosmologies for improved mental health, community building, and for the dismantling of oppressive colonial capitalistic systems. Their work as a trauma-informed peer support facilitator, crisis counselor, tropical and sidereal astrologer, sound healer, and medium, is guided by Mulema Alchemy. Mulema means heart in the Indigenous Sawa languages of her parents, and she believes in the transformative, alchemical power of the heart. Elmina is currently building a coalition devoted to ancestral Indigenous psychologies.

mulemaalchemy.wordpress.com

Fiona Wong

Fiona's journey with Human Design began as an act of resistance, a back-and-forth tugging of honoring who she "should" be due to upbringing and cultural obligations (she identifies as Chinese-Malaysian American) versus the person who she suppressed in order to navigate the world.

During this internal war, she learned to honor the communities and identities she came from while living as a continuation of the stories that she represents.

Respect for her individuality is the foundation of her renegade work with Human Design. The Wild Pixel is the vessel where she holds her writings and offerings through this system.

Fiona is a line 3/5 self-projected Projector incarnated through the vessel of love. She has a propensity for isolating herself and rewatching campy horror movies.

thewildpixel.com

Jasmine Nnenna

I am a philosopher, artist, and founder. For my astro folks, I'm a Capricorn Sun, Pisces Moon, Leo Rising. For my Human Design folks, I'm a 3/5 Pure Generator.

I am an advocate for the living philosophies of The Age of Awareness. It is a joy becoming fluent and supporting others in speaking the languages of awareness (Human Design, astrology, and Gene Keys) so that we can each break free from the society of sameness and into an era that centers our holistic wellness, humanity, and a more regenerative Earth.

Instagram @jasnnenna

Karen Curry Parker

Karen Curry Parker is a transformational teacher, speaker, and coach. She is a multiple bestselling author, EFT (emotional freedom techniques) practitioner since 2000, life coach since 1998, original student of Ra Uru Hu, and one of the world's leading Human Design teachers since 1999. She is also a Quantum University PhD student/guest lecturer and a TEDx presenter.

Karen is the founder and creator of two certification trainings, the Quantum Human Design™ for Everyone Training System and The Quantum Alignment System™ and is also the founder of the Understanding Human Design membership community. She is also the host of the *Quantum rEvolution Podcast* and co-founder of GracePoint Publishing.

Karen has a deep love for helping people activate their highest potential through teaching them how to consciously use language and narrative to increase their vitality and well-being, which in part is why she created Quantum Human Design™. Her core mission is to help people live the life they were designed to live by discovering who they are, what they are here to do, and how to activate their authentic life path by waking them up to the power of their innate creativity and unlimited possibility.

Karen is a 4/6 Time Bender (Manifesting Generator), mother of eight amazing humans, wife of a genius, and grandmother of two emerging world leaders. She has her BSN in nursing, BA in journalism and is currently working on her PhD in integrative health at Quantum University.

quantumhumandesign.com

About the Authors

Aycee Brown

Aycee Brown is a psychic channel, oracle, and voice of truth. Through spiritual guidance, she offers tools that inspire and motivate others to look at all parts of themselves so that they can develop the awareness to heal and show up in their lives fully.

Aycee knows that you were made for more than what you've been shown. Her unique wisdom and insight will allow you to step into the magical mother fucker you've always been. She does this through the lens of Human Design, astrology, numerology, psychic channeling, and mediumship.

Asha D Ramakrishna

Asha D Ramakrishna is a #1 bestselling author of the book *The Priestess Code: Awakening the Modern Woman* where Moon & Earth Principles are revealed for a more organic and harmonious approach to life, and co-author of *Your Soul Map: Liberation, Human Design, and the BIPOC Experience*. With a background in molecular biology and business development, she breaks esoteric teachings into practical logical approaches to living.

Asha is a Minister of Spiritual Peacemaking and she incorporates philosophies such as feng shui, karma healing, Human Design, to name a few. She is the founder of the Dharma School and Conscious Commerce Program. She is originally from Venezuela and of South Indian ancestry. She currently lives in occupied Nipmuc Land (Harvard, MA) with her soul mate, two human daughters, and a fifty-pound Portuguese water dog.

Work with Aycee and Asha!

Aycee Brown and Asha D Ramakrishna are available to provide their expertise to your organization.

Speaking Engagements: Keynotes, Event Panels, and Podcast Interviews covering the following topics:

- Spirituality
- Branding
- Marketing
- Corporate Communications

Consulting: building and structuring teams where individuals find fulfillment—teams work in synergy and organizations can meet their goals. Custom programs can be created for brands and corporations.

Human Design Workshops: A great addition to your wellness events or corporate retreat.

humandesignforliberation.com

For more great books from Human Design Press
Visit HumanDesignStore.com

HUMANDESIGN
PRESS

If you enjoyed reading *Your Soul Map: Liberation, Human Design, and the BIPOC Experience*, and purchased it through an online retailer, please return to the site and write a review to help others find the book.

Made in United States
Troutdale, OR
08/10/2023